DIY Bracelets Book

8 Friendship Bracelets Fun to Make, Wear and Share

Copyright © 2020

DEDICATION

Contents

Zig Zag Friendship Bracelet

Supplies needed to complete this friendship bracelet pattern:

Embroidery floss

Thread snippers

Measuring tape

Optional finishing supplies for making a zig zag friendship bracelet:

Ribbon crimps in the width of your bracelet

Flat nose pliers

Round nose pliers (or any second pair)

Clasp

Chain or a few jumprings to connect clasp to

Jumprings for attaching ribbon crimp to clasp

Instructions:

. Choose at least 4 colors to create an ombre/gradient plus your joker color (that won't show)

. Cut them to size. The approximate measurements are as follows (toss in an extra inch or two if you know you'll need every last bit of the full length).

For a 4-color gradient (joker, then darkest to lightest, in inches): 13, 18, 27, 36, 45

For a 7-color gradient: 16, 22, 33, 42, 51, 60, 69, 78.

If you're really ambitious, you can probably do a few more shades, adding +9 inches for each one, and adding an extra 3-6 inches per color for the earlier shades.

. Place them in order from shortest to longest – first the joker, then the darkest, and each descending shade until you reach the white or almost white strand.

. Knot your strands together about 1 inch from the end if you plan

3

to add a clasp, 2 inches if you plan to tie it on your wrist.

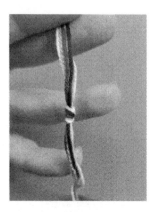

. Optional: tape it down to your surface.

The order of your strands may have shifted slightly so make sure to separate them and place them in order before knotting your first row. By the way, the bracelet is flipped over – in step 3 I did it darkest to lightest, however when I taped it down, I flipped it over so that I worked lightest to darkest. Just an oversight... doesn't really matter!

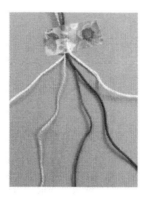

. Start by knotting your lightest strand around the one to its right.

In case you're not familiar with this kind of knot, here's a photo:

Pull it up to the top of your bracelet.

. Knot again around the same thread. This double knot forms a "stitch" on the front of your zig zag friendship bracelet. The entire bracelet pattern is made of these stitches. This direction is called a "forward knot".

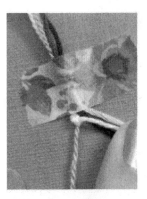

. Continue with the forward knot using the white string around the other strings in the correct order, finishing with the joker.

. Take your second lightest color, which should now be the leftmost strand. Forward knot it around the other strings – skipping the lightest color. Here's a little trick to remember what to do: you never wrap a string around one that's lighter than it in the ombre. You always finish your row with the joker.

Continue with this process, with each row one shorter than the one above, until you've done every string besides the joker and your last row had one stitch (your darkest color).

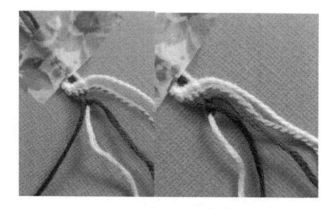

0.You've completed half a round! Time to hit "rewind" (I'm really giving myself away as a 90's girl here...)

Tie your rightmost string (the lightest) around the one to its left. Tie again to create a double knot/stitch. This is called a backward knot.

Continue double knotting your other strings, from right to left — like you did in step 8 but reversed.

1. Continue the process of step 9 in reverse, backward knotting all your strings around those darker than them, finishing with the "joker". You've now completed a whole round!

2. Repeat steps 6-11, until you're satisfied with the length of your zig zag friendship bracelet.

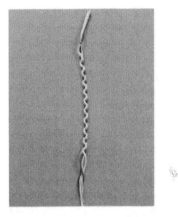

3.Knot the end and trim! You can tie it directly on to your wrist if you'd like.

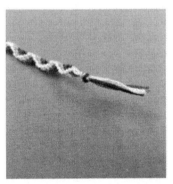

4.Or, add a clasp! To do this, bury your knots in ribbon crimps (you may need to widen the openings on the crimps first) and close them tightly. Trim any threads that are sticking out. Add a clasp and connector and wear with pride!

You can see the radical difference between a four-color gradient and a seven-color one!

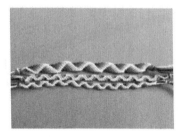

Fancy Friendship Bracelets

Materials:

3 strips of fabric, 10" long by .75" wide

Jewelry Endcaps

Glue

1. Cut 3 strips of fabric 3/4" wide by 10" long. *Use 1" wide strips for a thicker variation

2. Fold long edges of strips in so they meet in the middle. Press.

3. Fold strip in half so the raw edges are enclosed. Press well.

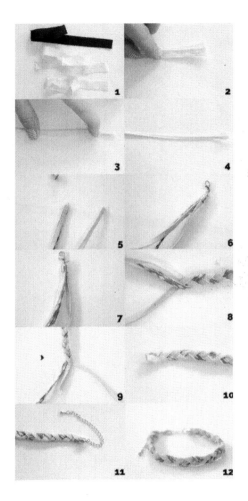

4. Stitch strip to secure. Repeat with all 3 strips.

5. Glue ends of strips together with a dab of glue between each one. Create a stack.

6. Glue end of stack into endcap hardware.

7. Press into the hardware as far as it will go and let dry.

8. Braid strips. Continue until your bracelet is the desired length.

9. When it is as long as you want, glue ends together.

10. Clip ends.

11. Glue other side into the other side of jewelry hardware.

12. Clip the bracelet together and you're done!

For a thicker bracelet (like the green, blue and purple one above)

use 1" wide strips.

Braided Friendship Bracelets

SUPPLIES

Embroidery thread in the colors of your choice

Letter beads

Buttons

Scissors

Tape to secure your thread

INSTRUCTIONS

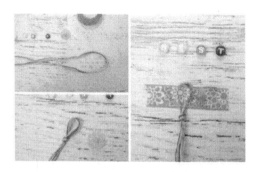

1. First, you want to measure out your string. I used my daughter's wrist as a guide and cut our string to 4x the length around her wrist. You will need 3 pieces cut to this length.

Fold your string in half and tie a loop knot at one end. Make your loop big enough to fit your button, but not too big that the button will come undone easily.

Tape down the end of your string to a table.

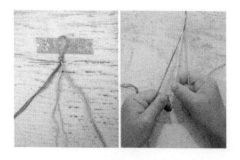

2. Separate your string into 3 groups, so you will have 2 pieces of string in each group. Start braiding your bracelet.

My daughter was able to braid on her own but did need some help keeping her braid tight enough.

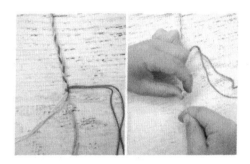

3. Once you reach a bit less than half way, you can string on your letter beads.

We made 2 sets of friendship bracelets, here are some ideas for your letter beads:

Best / Friends

BFFS / Besties

Friends / Forever

BFFS / Forever

You could even make a set of 3: Best / Friends / Forever

Kids can also spell their names or the names of their friends.

Before you start stringing on your letter beads you need to tie a knot where you stopped braiding. String your letter beads onto the middle 2 pieces of string.

When you are finished, you will need to tie another knot. Some kids might need help tying their knots.

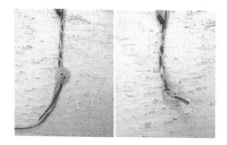

4. Continue braiding until you reach the desired size of your bracelet.

5. Thread 2 or more pieces of string through your button. On the buttons that have 4 holes, you can pass the thread through a couple of times.

Tie a knot at the back of the button and trim off the excess thread like in the picture above.

These braided friendship bracelets turned out so cute! They make such a fun activity for kids to make for their friends as a special handmade gift.

The design possibilities are endless with different colored thread, fun shaped buttons, and different words. Each bracelet will be totally unique!

Friendship Bracelets For Adults

Materials Needed:

Embroidery floss in colors of your choice

Ring clasp (from toggle clasp set) and lobster clasp

Needle (eye should be large enough to fit one piece of embroidery floss

Scissors

Charms or rhinestone embellishments (optional...see end of tutorial for more info)

Step 1:

Cut 6 strands of floss (3 of each color) into 70-inch pieces. Thread all of the strands through the small hole in the circular end of the round clasp. Tie a knot to secure the clasp directly in the center of the strands. Tape the metal circle to your working surface, and divide the floss on either side so that each side mirrors one another.

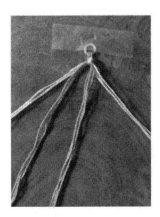

Step 2:

Begin knotting according to the instructions for the chevron bracelet.**Don't forget to tie each knot twice. I forgot when I started, and as you can see in the photo below, the knots in the first four sections are too thin. Oops.

Step 3:

Keep knotting until the bracelet is the right length for your wrist.

To make it easier, measure your wrist and cut a string the same length as your wrist to use as a guide. Don't forget to factor in the length of the clasps!

Step 4:

When the bracelet is at the perfect length, slide the lobster clasp onto the end. Before we secure the lobster clasp, we're going to add some extra floss to make a tassel. This isn't necessary, but it adds a little pizazz and also helps conceal the knot and loose strands you'd otherwise be left with.

Step 5:

To make the tassel, cut about 12 strands of floss into 6" pieces. These extra strands can be the same colors you used for your bracelet or a different color. In this tutorial I used orange.

Lay the tassel strands horizontally across the bracelet strands, just beneath the lobster clasp as shown.

Step 6.

Gather all of the bracelet strands (the white and pink ones in this example) and tie them together in a knot at the base of the lobster clasp, securing the tassel strands inside the knot.

Step 7:

Taking another piece of embroidery floss, tie a knot at the base of the big knot (see below). I slid on a little rhinestone charm before I tied the knot, but this is totally optional.

Step 8:

After you've tied the knot, wrap the piece of floss around the base of the big knot tightly several times. Thread one of the ends of the floss through the needle and draw it back through the wrapped strands and through the center of the knot to secure it. Trim the end so it's invisible.

Repeat with the other loose end.

Step 9.

Trim the tassel to your desired length, making sure the ends are even. Use your fingers to separate the strands to make the tassel look fuller.

If you don't want to add any additional embellishments, you're all done! If you would like to add some colored rhinestones to the front of the bracelet, continue reading below.

How to Add Rhinestones to a Friendship Bracelet:

To add rhinestones, look for a "rhinestone chain" at either your local craft store or jewelry making store. You can usually find them in opaque colors or clear.

Cut the rhinestone chain to the length of your bracelet. Thread a piece of embroidery floss that matches or complements your bracelet onto the needle. Tie a knot at the end of the thread so that it will be secure when you start sewing.

Starting at the underside of the bracelet, begin sewing the rhinestone chain onto the center of the bracelet by sewing the thread in between the rhinestones. If you want to go over each section more than once to completely conceal the metal, you can, but once is enough to secure it to the bracelet.

After you've finished sewing on the rhinestones, turn the bracelet over and thread the floss through the loops in the back. Tie it in a knot to secure it, and trim the ends.

You're finished!

How to Add a charm to a friendship bracelet:

If you'd like to add a charm, like the little bird in the photo below, calculate where the middle of the bracelet will be. When you've knotted to that point, simply slide the charm onto the thread at the far right before and continue knotting as before.

These bracelets are fun to make, and fun to wear. Wear them alone, or pair them with other string or metal bracelets. Share them with a friend, or keep them for yourself. Blast some 80's music in the background and take a fun trip down memory lane, while making pretty jewelry in the process.

Diy Braided Friendship Bracelets

What you need to make braided friendship bracelets:

28

Baker's twine in your favorite colors

2 Ribbon end crimps

3 Twisted jump rings or an inch of twisted cable chain

Two pairs of jewelry making pliers: One chain nose, and another of your choice. (I just used my round nose and chain nose pliers.)

A clasp that opens wide enough to fit over your jump rings or cable chain easily.

How to make braided friendship bracelets:

. Cut six pieces of twine, about a foot in length.

. Use a ribbon crimp end to attach your threads. Mae sure that they are all lined up neatly in the crimp end. You may want to use one slightly wider than your twines – it will be easier. Crimp it in place using chain nose pliers.

. Split your strings into three sets of two.

. And start braiding.

. When you're halfway through, if you want, you can make a double knot, just for fun.

. Continue braiding until the bracelet is long enough to fit your wrist.

. Trim the strings, but be careful that your braid doesn't come apart!

. Crimp your second half the same way you did the first. You can see that I struggled to keep my string inside the ribbon crimps, though it did work out in the end. That's because I used ones that are too narrow. I highly recommend using a wider one, especially if this is your first time using these.

. Attach a spring ring or lobster claw clasp to one end.

0.On the other end, you can attach a piece of cable chain, or a few pretty jump rings to make an adjustable closure. When you open jump rings, make sure to open them in a forward-backward motion, not side-to-side, so that you don't weaken it.

Attach the first jump ring to the hole on the crimp.

Attach another one to that, and then a third one at the end, to make a three-loop "chain".

Your bracelets are ready to wear!

Diy: Friendship Bracelets For Beginners

What you'll need:

3 different colors of embroidery floss

Scissors

Some tape or a safety pin

1. Cut Your Thread

First choose the colors of your bracelet. You can use anywhere from 2 to 10 different colors. If this is your first friendship bracelet, I suggest using 2 or 3 colors. I have chosen to use 3. Cut a strand of each color that's about 32 inches long.

2. Securing Your String

Holding all the strings together, tie a knot, leaving about 3 inches above the knot. Then secure the strings so that you can begin your bracelet. You can either use a safety pin to pin it to your jeans or you can tape it to a table or book.

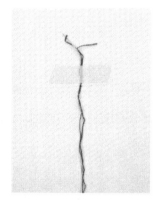

3. Choose Your First Color

Separate your first color from the rest of the strands. With your starting string on your left side and the rest of the strings held together on your right, take your left string and cross it over the right strings, making the shape of a number 4.

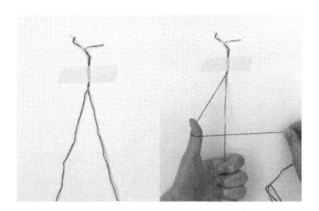

4. Tying The Knot

Then loop the left strand under the right strands and through the middle of your number 4 shape. Pull the end up firmly to complete the knot. Repeat steps 3 and 4 with the same string for as long as you want that color to be.

5. Changing Colors

When you're ready to change colors, take the next color from your right hand and trade it with your left. With your new color in your left hand, repeat steps 3 and 4 until ready to change colors again. Continue to change colors until you reach the end of your bracelet, leaving about 3 inches at the end.

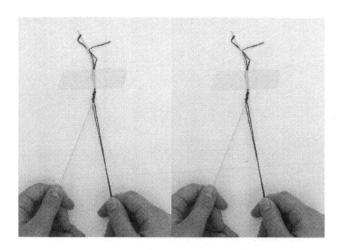

6. Finishing

I like to finish the ends of my friendship bracelets by dividing the strings into 3 groups and braiding both ends.

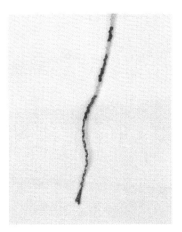

7. Ta da!

You have finished your friendship bracelet. If you make yours with a friend, you can both trade and wear each other's. You can also make two matching bracelets for both you and your friend to wear. Once you get the hang of making these feel free to add more colors! My favorite number is 6 different colors, but you can have as many as you want.

Macraméd Friendship Bracelets

Materials

Since this is such a free form enterprise the amount of colors of DMC embroidery floss you get is really up to you. We used a package of the DMC Light Effects Fluorescent Embroidery Floss and then picked our individual colors around them. Here is a list of the individual colors we used: Ecru, Blanco, 155, 156, 157, 307, 445, 453, 606, 648, 666, 712, 746, 906, 907, 956, 3033, 3761, 3843.

Please not that the fluorescent thread is slightly thicker than the regular DMC floss. So if you are mixing the two together it works best if you pull out and discard one ply of the fluorescent thread.

Beginning

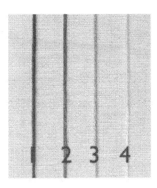

To begin, pick out your colors. For the purposes of this how-to and the following patterns each color will be assigned a number.

For patterns use a doubled length of thread cut each color to a length of 72-inches. Hold the cut pieces together, fold them in half, and then make a 3/4-inch long slip knot at the fold.

Using a safety pin pin the loop to your jeans (or any other stable piece of fabric that you don't mind getting holes in) to keep it steady.

Arrange the threads as instructed in the pattern. In the example above the thread order would be: 1, 2, 3, 4, 4, 3, 2, 1

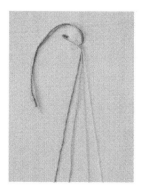

For patterns that use a single length of thread cut a 36-inch length from each color. Arrange the pieces in the proper order. Leaving a 6-inch tail, tie a simple overhand knot to start.

The left knot

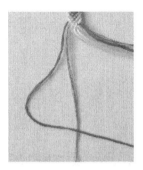

Place a piece of thread (in this case thread #1) over the piece thread to its right (in this case thread #2) in a sort of a "4" shape as shown above

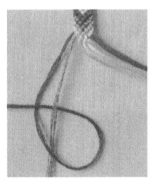

Pull the end of the thread through this "4" loop creating a knot.

While holding the right thread taut pull up the left thread to form a tight knot as shown above. Repeat once more. Both the Left and Right Knots are actually made up of two knots each.

If you are tying more than one Left Knot in a row you will use the same thread (in this case thread #1) to tie the subsequent knots along the a row from left to right.

Right knot

The right knot is made in the same manner as the left but in the opposite direction.

Place a piece of thread over its left hand neighbor in the "P" shape shown above.

Pull the thread's end through the "P" to form a knot.

While pulling the left thread tightly down pull the right thread up to form a taut knot. Repeat this once to make a full Right Knot. Remember both the left and right knots are actually made up of two knots each.

If you are tying more than one Right Knot in a row you will use the same thread (in this case thread 1) to tie the subsequent knots along the row from right to left.

Ending

There are a couple of good ways to end your friendship bracelets.

To end a bracelet that starts with a loop separate the threads into two equal groups. Braid each group and tie a knot at the end trimming the ends to be neat and short.

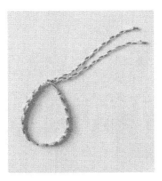

To wear pull the ends though the starting loop and tie a knot.

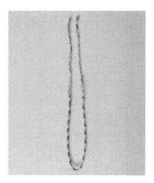

To end a bracelet that starts with a knot tie another knot at the end of the macramé. Braid both ends and tied knots. Trim to ends to look neat.

To wear tie the ends together in a bow.

PATTERNS

Basic stripes

1. Use a single length of thread and any amount of colors you like. Arrange the color in a pleasing order.

2. Starting at the far left tie a row of Left Knots using the 1st color across the whole width of the bracelet.

3. Repeat step 2 until the bracelet is the desired length.

Chevron

1. Using doubled thread and at least 3 colors arrange the threads in a mirror image. For instance, if you were using six colors as in the example above you would arrange the threads like this: 1, 2, 3, 4, 5, 6, 6, 5, 4, 3, 2, 1.

2. Starting at the far left side make a row of left knots stopping in the middle of the bracelet when the colors start repeating. For instance, in the six color example above you would tie five left knots.

3. Starting at the far right side tie a row of right knots to the middle. When you get to the middle of the bracelet you will meet up with the thread from step 2. Tie this with a right knot as well. You will always be tying one more knot in step 3 than in step 2. For instance in the six color example above you would tie six right knots in step 3.

4. Repeat steps 2 and 3 until the bracelet is the desired length.

As another option you can change the arrangement of the threads in step one to make a more varied and braided looking bracelet.

Diamonds

The diamond shape is the most complicated one I tackled so here are a step by step instructions to make a 4 color bracelet. Once you get the idea with the 4 color version you explore thinner or wider versions as well.

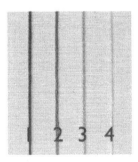

Here are the four threads and their corresponding numbers.

Using doubled strands start the bracelet with a loop and arrange the colors in a mirror image: colors 1, 2, 3, 4, 4, 3, 2, 1.

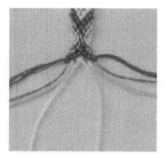

Start by tying a left knot with both strands of color 4 in the center.

Please note, these photos start at the middle of the bracelet just because it's easier to see the pattern that way.

Then, starting with the right hand thread 4 strand tie a row of 3 left knots as shown above.

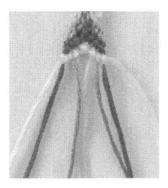

Next take the other thread 4 strand from the middle and tie a row three right knots as shown above. This shape will be called the upside down "V" in this pattern.

In this same manner make upside down "V"s with colors 3, 2, and 1 always starting from the center and moving out.

When you get back to color 4 make a left knot in the center.

Using the right hand piece of thread 4 make a right knot with the thread directly to the right.

Using the left hand piece of thread 4 make a left knot with the thread directly to the left.

Tie the two color 4 pieces together with a left knot.

With color 1 make a "V" shape just as you would for the chevron pattern: Starting from the far left side tie a row of 3 left knots. Then, starting from the far right side tie a row of 4 right knots to form the "V" shape.

Make another "V" shape with color 2.

Starting at the far left tie two left knots with color 3.

Starting at the far right side tie two right knots with color 3.

At the far left side tie a right knot with color 4.

At the far right side tie a left knot with color 4.

With the left strand of color 3 tie two right knots in a row to

the strands of colors 1 and 4 directly the left.

Do the reverse for the other side: with the right strand of color 3 tie two left knots.

Tie an upside down "V" shape with color 2.

Tie an upside down "V" shape starting with color 1.

Now you're back at the beginning.

Repeat this until the bracelet is the desired length.

Once you get the hang of all the patterns you can mix and match them like we did in the green bracelet above.

Diy Friendship Bracelets: Fishtail Braid.

All you need for this project is some embroidery floss. Also, the tiny delicate bracelet is a new fave from gorjana.

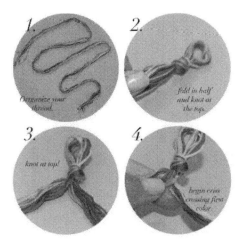

1. Organize your thread. You'll need three forty inch strands of floss, in 5 colors (15 total strands.)

2. Fold bundle of floss in half, and carefully knot at the top, forming a loop. You'll want your loop to be large enough later to wrap the ends through to tie it on to your wrist.

3. Sort your thread. On each side, there should be three strands of each of your five colors. Keep each color together.

4. Begin the bracelet by criss-crossing the first color (bundle of three strands,) over to the opposite side.

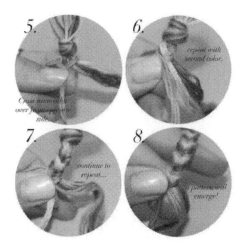

5. Continue the bracelet by crossing the same color over from the opposite side.

6. Repeat steps 4 and 5 with your next color. Note – it won't look very pretty at first.

7. Continue to repeat steps 4 and 5 with every color, keeping the floss tight and organized.

8. A really beautiful chevron pattern will emerge!

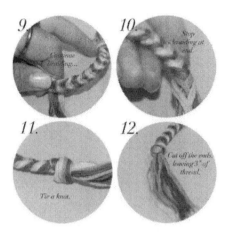

9. Continue to braid until you reach your desired length.

10. Stop braiding. (Is this even really a step?)

11. Tie a knot.

12. Leaving about 3 inches of floss, trim the ends. You're all done!

16458300R00038

Business Ethics: A Christian Method for Making Moral Decisions

John K. Tarwater, Ph.D.

Coram Deo Publishing
Cedarville, OH 45314

Please send your comments about this book to:
jtarwater@cedarville.edu

Coram Deo Publishing
Cedarville, OH

ISBN: (Paperback)
978-0-9982392-2-4

Printed in the United States of America

Contents

Preface

My first introduction to the business world occurred before I was even a teenager. Growing up in a small, rural town in East Tennessee, I sold gallons of blackberries that I had picked from bushes that surrounded our home and barn. This entrepreneurial endeavor allowed me to earn approximately $12 per gallon in 1980. At ten years of age, I assumed that I would get rich soon if I continued at this rate! Over the next few summers, I slowly moved away from picking blackberries to pursuing other avenues for making money. I picked-up trash at the local city park; I bussed tables and washed dishes for a restaurant; I worked for a general contractor; and in college, I hauled hay for a local farmer. Thus, I learned from an early age the value of hard work and saving.

Academically and professionally, I expanded these early lessons in business. I received a bachelor's degree in business administration. After passing the Certified Public Accounting (CPA) examination, I worked as a tax accountant for a midsized public accounting firm in Dallas, Texas. Later, I also completed doctoral studies in finance. Although each of these events expanded my knowledge and understanding of how the world of business technically operates, I never outgrew or strayed from my initial education gained from my time of picking blackberries around the barn.

My exposure to ethics was similar. My parents and church taught me the importance of honesty, stewardship, and giving, but a formal introduction to the field of ethics did not occur until my graduate studies at Duke University. Stephen Long, who now serves as the Cary M. Maguire Professor of Ethics at Southern Methodist University, taught me in Introduction to Christian Ethics.[1] While at Duke, I also took classes on War and the Christian Tradition with Stanley Hauerwas and on New Testament Ethics with Richard Hays.[2] Eventually, I completed a doctoral degree in Christian Ethics at Southeastern Baptist Theological Seminary under the tutelage of Dan Heimbach. Graduate studies in ethics greatly enhanced my ability to think ethically and to see the essential connection between how one thinks (i.e., worldview) and how one discerns what is morally good or evil. Like my early education in business, I never deviated from the moral instruction I received from my parents and the church.

Because of my formal training in business and ethics, I have the opportunity to teach classes at the university level in business ethics. From this platform, I have had the opportunity to explore in detail the historic link between these two fields, as well as how Christian Scriptures should shape one's thinking with regard to them. This book represents my first attempt at formally engaging in this important conversation.

I enter this discussion fully cognizant that it has a rather extensive history. Adam Smith is considered by many the father of capitalism due to the impact of his book, *The Wealth of Nations*.[3] But Smith's understanding of economics is not disconnected from the world of ethics. To the contrary, it flows from his moral philosophy which he expounded in his earlier publication, *The Theory of Moral Sentiments*.[4] Smith is unable to divorce the virtues of the moral individual in his *Moral Sentiments* from the principles of justice and law at work in the economic realm discussed in *The Wealth of Nations*.

Smith is not the only one to recognize this integral connection between economics and ethics. Early twentieth century authors often couched the conversation in terms of welfare economics. In his *The Economic Problem*, British economist Ralph Hawtrey wrote: "But economics cannot be disassociated from ethics. Those who say that wealth or utility is the end of economic action are committing themselves to ethical propositions, which are open to challenge and need to be defended and justified."[5] Nobel laureate, Joseph Stigler added:

> At the level of economic policy, then, it is totally misleading to talk of ends as individual and random; they are fundamentally collective and organized. If this conclusion be accepted, and accept it we must, the economist may properly exceed the narrow confines of economic analysis. He may cultivate a second discipline, the determination of the ends of his society

particularly relevant to economic policy. This discipline might be called, following J. N. Keynes, applied ethics.[6]

Clearly, some early economists could not imagine separating ethics and economics.

Business ethics, although clearly related to economics ethics, developed somewhat independently. One of the earliest attempts to integrate ethical thinking into the business discipline came at the hand of Edgar Heermance, who in 1926 published his book *The Ethics of Business: A Study of Current Standards.*[7] Since Heermance's publication, the field of business ethics has grown greatly with various business organizations and journals coming to life. The *Society for Business Ethics*, for instance, started in 1980. Also, several journals on the topic began publication: the *Journal of Business Ethics* (JBE) began in 1982 and *European Business Ethics Network* began publication in 1987.[8]

Within the field of business ethics, authors and practitioners have struggled to develop a single unifying approach. Some of the earliest efforts focused almost exclusively on corporate social responsibilities (CSR), suggesting that corporations have an obligation to society at large that should go beyond mere legal liability.[9] Bowen offered the first formal definition of the movement writing: "It refers to the obligations of businessmen to pursue those policies, to make those decisions, or to follow those lines of action which are desirable in terms of the objectives and values of our society."[10] But this responsibility was not viewed as antithetical to the profit motive. To the contrary, authors within the movement assumed that businesses should use CSR opportunities to extend economic benefit.[11]

By 1990s, business ethics had begun to transition from CSR to alternative themes, such as stakeholder theory. Stakeholder theory recognizes that businesses have numerous stakeholders, such as employees, suppliers, creditors, and others. As part of a strategic approach to management, Freeman argued that managers must keep in mind their responsibility to these competing stakeholders.[12] In a subsequent publication, he made clear that moral responsibility is part of one's obligation to stakeholders.[13]

Not everyone was pleased with Freeman's decision to mix a manager's responsibility to maximize profit with ethical discourse. Kuhn and Shriver, for example, challenge Freeman's suggestion that business owners need to manage stakeholder relationships.[14] Additionally, Kenneth Goodpaster, former professor at Notre Dame and Harvard Business School, criticized stakeholder theory. He said that "stakeholder analysis" unnecessarily creates a paradox between one's fiduciary responsibility to various stakeholders and one's moral obligation to the owner.[15] More to the point, Boatright insists: "It is illegitimate to orient corporate decisions that bear on the fiduciary duties of management by ethical values that go beyond strategic stakeholder considerations to include the interests of other constituencies, but it is essential to orient other corporate decisions by these values."[16] Ultimately, Freeman argued that it is impossible to separate the domains of business and ethics. He argued that when one speaks with stakeholders or stockholders, one is engaging in discourse that is normative, descriptive, and instrumental.[17] In order to provide a normative core to stakeholder theory, Freeman proposed what he called the "Doctrine of Fair Contracts," which attempted to couch rights of the various stakeholders in moral categories.[18]

Although various authors continue to appeal to stakeholder theory in their works on business ethics, it has largely lost some of its early popularity. Even Freeman himself has argued that there does not exist a normative stakeholder theory, but rather a general framework for management that includes various ethical structures for "stakeholder analysis."[19]

What should be clear from this brief survey of the history of business and ethics is that each of these popular approaches to the literature have serious shortcomings. First, whether one is speaking of welfare economics, a business' corporate responsibility, or a business' moral responsibility to its stakeholders, all references to God and Scripture are completely absent. Consequently, each of these models represent humanly devised attempts to arrive at a universal moral norms. But this type of approach always fails. To be sure, when God is removed from ethical discourse, morality necessarily loses any fixed norms, which leads to the second major critique.

Because speculative approaches to business ethics has no fixed moral foundation, it necessarily becomes relative and changing. Even though he argued for fair contracts as a normative core, Freeman recognized that multiple normative frameworks existed and that one was not necessarily superior to others. He contended for what he called "reasonable pluralism."[20] Some authors remove all doubt concerning the relative nature of their approach. In her *Business Ethics*, Paliwal presents various difficult issues in business ethics to which she argues there are "no clear-cut right answers."[21] Indeed, the majority of texts for business ethics present a various ethical theories, including utilitarian, Kantian, rights, and virtue ethics, but present them as if all are equally valid.[22]

Lastly, most secular approaches to business ethics ignore meta-ethical issues and overly focus on dilemmas and case studies. By ignoring metaphysical and epistemological concepts, these texts fail to provide readers with the philosophical foundations that allow them to interact with perennial concerns that undergird ethical issues.[23] Questions of right and wrong are not new. They have been the subject of discourse since the beginning of time. But every moral claim is simultaneously an evaluation about one's self and the issue under question. That is, values and judgments do not arise out of thin air. Rather, they simply reflect one's worldview— their conception of God, reality, knowledge, and ethics. Thus, any approach to ethics that ignores this reality does not adequately prepare the reader for broader ethical evaluation.

In recent years, some very good works have been produced that seek to deal with these shortcomings. Richard Chewning edited a three-volume series entitled, *Christians in the Marketplace*.[24] Few works could rival the theological depth that the authors bring to these essays. Each author appears to take seriously the application of Scripture to the issues under evaluation, and each volume seeks to deal with both pragmatic and meta-ethical issues. However, the audience for the material seems to be more appropriate for theologians who are seeking to understand better the application of their field to business than the student of business who is pursuing application of biblical truth to their field. Stated differently, the essays are written at a theological level that make it difficult for many students graduating from colleges of business to access and apply the material well.

Other texts also recognize the authority of Scripture in ethical evaluation in the marketplace. One of the older texts, *Business through the Eyes of Faith*, introduces the student to business ethics from a Christian perspective. It treats a few broad business concepts through the lens of Scripture and deals with some deeper concepts, like justice, love, and humility.[25] Similarly, Alexander Hill, a professor of business and economics at Seattle Pacific University, explored how the business student might rightly apply the Christian concepts of holiness, just, and love to issues encountered in the world of business. In the opening pages, the author does a good job of highlighting God's character, as revealed in Scripture, as the foundation for ethics in business.[26]

More recently, two authors in particular have expanded the conversation between the domains of business and ethics. In *Beyond Integrity*, authors Scott Rae and Kenman Wong present the reader with primary texts from various authors dealing with many of the issues that I covered in my historical survey, such as stakeholder theory and corporate social responsibility. [27] The authors blend well the more difficult philosophical and ethical issues with more concrete and pragmatic issues. Perhaps better than any other text, the authors grapple with the authority of Scripture to issues in business ethics.

Michael Cafferky, the Ruth McKee Chair for Entrpreneurship and Business Ethics at Southern Adventist University, has also written an excellent text on business ethics. He too writes from a Christian perspective. In his work, he applies twelve biblical themes to various contemporary issues in different fields of business, such as management, accounting, marketing, and global business. He also presents some alternative theories to ethics, such as utilitarianism, virtue ethics, and rights, to name a few.

With some of these more recent works on business ethics from a Christian perspective, one might question the need for another text like the present volume. Most texts on business ethics attempt to introduce the student to a considerable number of case studies where the student works through various dilemmas. Although most of the texts address some foundational issues, it is clear that the majority of authors focus their works on being "practical." Because of the scarcity of attention given to ethical methodology through which one grapples with meta-ethical issues, students in many business ethics classes are ill prepared to be "practical." That is, they do not know HOW to do ethics.

In the classes of business ethics that I teach at Cedarville University, I too have students deal with pressing issues in the business world from a Christian perspective. However, we do not fully interact with these issues until later in the semester—only after I have had the opportunity to present to them critical foundational truths. This text reflects my approach to these foundational concepts. It is my understanding of HOW one does business ethics from a Christian perspective.

As with any book, many individuals contributed their time and expertise in order to make this publication possible. Several colleagues at Cedarville read parts of all of this manuscript and offered corrections and helpful insights. I especially want to thank J.R. Gilhooly and Josh Kira. Additionally, I am grateful to the numerous students that have taken my classes over the years and have improved the text through their questions and comments. Despite the contributions of many, it is likely that the perceptive reader will still discover some errors in the following pages, and of course, they are solely the responsibility of the author.

John K. Tarwater
Cedarville University
Cedarville, OH
June 2019

Chapter 1:
Introductory Questions

Why should one study ethics?

Recently, I began my business ethics classes by placing two objects in front of the class: a jar of jelly beans and a palette of colors. Then, I asked various students to respond to two questions: how many jelly beans are in the jar and what is your favorite color? After several students had participated, I would call on a different student and ask: "Which guess about the number of jelly beans is correct?" Usually, the student would respond with something like: "I am not sure, but I think the one who said such-and-such number is probably closest." Afterwards, I asked the student, "With regard to the second question, which answer do you think is correct?" The student immediately responds, "There is no wrong answer. Everyone is correct." Finally, I ended the discussion with one final question: "Is the study of ethics more like question one (the number of jelly beans in a jar) or question two (one's favorite color)?" In every class, about nine out of ten students responded that ethics is like choosing one's favorite color.

In other words, students (even at conservative, evangelical universities) largely consider the issues related to ethics to be subjective and relative. Their responses remind me of an incident that occurred when I was teaching ethics and theology at another university. A couple of colleagues and I began a round table discussion with professors in the science department. We would meet one day per week to discuss chapters from Lee Strobel's book, *Case for a Creator*.[1] The aim of the discussion was to encourage open dialog between the members of the science and Christian studies departments. We were hoping that the science professors would better understand the bases of our conclusions about scientific issues and that we might likewise comprehend more fully the substance of their positions on the same issues. After the group had been meeting for several weeks and had entertained a number of theories about creation from both a theological and scientific perspective, one of the science professors made a powerfully revealing statement. The professor was attempting to make a positive statement about the contribution of the theology professors to the discussions. However, his statement revealed more about his misunderstanding of the theological discipline than it did to encourage my colleagues and me. He stated, "I always thought professors of theology were glorified Sunday school teachers."

The science professor's statement was shocking on several points. As professors of theology, we had completed doctoral studies in our fields just as the professors of chemistry and biology had completed doctoral studies in their disciplines. Similarly, we were required to be familiar with the professional literature of our field, pass exams not only in our primary fields, but also in cognate areas including exams in German and Latin. In addition, each of us had published books and articles in academically recognized areas. Knowing this, what would have led the professor to make such a statement about professional theologians?

Interestingly, I am convinced that this professor's opinion is not unique. Rather, I think his opinion reflects a common perception that people hold about religious and ethical reflection. Namely, ethics and theology are like choosing one's favorite color and, therefore, they do not require the academic rigor associated with evaluating issues in the hard sciences. When it comes to ethics, therefore, people might ask: "Why do we need to study ethics? Don't people really intuitively know what is right and wrong?" For the most part, the majority of the populace would agree about a number of ethical conclusions. Most people consider actions like murder and stealing to be evil and wrong. So, why formally study ethics?

To Live Rightly before God

When one looks at myriad of contemporary ethical issues confronting business executives, one quickly realizes that everyone does not know intuitively what is right and wrong. Rather, one recognizes just how much the average person approaches ethics like they would their favorite color: today's answer might change because it is not grounded in anything more than one's opinion.[2] Consider, for example, the Affordable Care Act's requirement that insurance plans cover preventive services, which the Health and Human Services (HHS) department interpreted the Act to mean employers must cover 18 separate methods of contraception used by women. When "Obamacare" was first passed, some praised the new mandates about contraception using moral language. Others, like Hobby Lobby and religious universities, complained and similarly used moral language. These moral disagreements show that not everyone agrees regarding what is right and wrong.

> **Exercise 1.1**: Identify at least two companies that objected to the mandate of contraceptive coverage for employees. Then respond to the question: On what moral basis would a company object to providing contraceptive coverage for its employees? Be sure to couch your responses in moral terms and not in financial or political terms. ∎

A second major ethical issue in business ethics that has captured the attention of numerous politicians concerns minimum wage. In classes on economics, we often discuss the consequences of raising federal minimum wage levels. To be sure, economic theory fairly unanimously agrees that a price floor above the equilibrium level results in an excess of labor demanded (i.e., an increase in unemployment). What is most important for our discussion, however, is how many of the discussions about minimum wage have begun to be couched in moral terms. Writing for *The Atlantic*, for example, Norm Ornstein published an article entitled, "The Moral and Economic Imperative to Raise the Minimum Wage."[3] On the other hand, author and ethicist Ben Crenshaw published an article entitled, "The Moral

Argument against the Minimum Wage."[4] Again, it does not appear that everyone agrees on what is right and wrong.

As Christians, we desperately desire to live in a manner that elicits God's praise. The study of ethics helps us to understand which actions, attitudes, and thoughts please God (and thus are good and right). Writing to the church at Ephesus, the apostle Paul claimed that we are created by God "for good works" (Eph. 2:10). Thus, the study of ethics assists individuals in identifying "good works": what is morally right and what is morally wrong. When Martin Luther was asked to recant at the Diet of Worms in 1521, he famously stated that unless he was convinced by the testimony of Scriptures or by clear reason, he could not retract his words. "Here I stand; I cannot do otherwise." Luther stated that the reason he could not recant was because it was not safe to go against one's "conscience." Luther based his understanding of conscience on the idea that all of humanity exists *coram deo*—before the presence of God. Our entire life takes place not only before God, but under his authority. The Psalmist rightly notes that there is no place that we can go to escape God's presence (Ps. 139). Our life and our life's decisions are always being appraised by the Moral Ruler of the universe. And for that reason, all of life is necessarily moral. Because all of life is *coram deo*, ethical study and reflection are important. Such reflection helps us to understand what actions God deems morally praise-worthy and those which He considers wrong (c.f. 1 Peter 3:13 – 17).

To Meet Academic Requirements

One may study ethics, therefore, to better understand and recognize what actions are good or evil from a Christian perspective. However, one may simply say, "I am taking ethics because it is required for my major." If this is the case, one might wonder WHY it is required. Why do so many majors in the fields of business (e.g., accounting, finance, marketing, management, information technology, etc.) require students to complete courses in ethics? For the most part, the move toward requiring ethics in various fields arose several years ago when a plethora of high-profile cases involving ethical lapses occurred: Enron, WorldCom, Arthur Anderson, and Adelphia Communications. In the wake of such catastrophic cases, most professional fields of study concluded its members needed more training in the areas of ethics. Although ethical study may be required in your academic preparation, the requirement itself arose from the fact that more and more individuals appeared to be operating in the business world in unethical manners. Hence, even when individuals seemed to know the difference between right and wrong, they appeared to still be choosing wrongly. Consequently, formal training in ethics has become a commonplace practice within schools of business.

To Understand the Basis for WHY an Action is Morally Right

The formal study of ethics is also important because it helps people to identify the basis for WHY they believe an action is right or wrong. One may be convinced that the requirement that employers provide contraceptive coverage for their employees is morally wrong, but they may struggle to identify the reasons for such a "gut feeling." Ethics provides individuals with the tools to analyze and understand the nature of ethical behavior, helping people to not only identify what actions are good and evil, but more importantly to understand why. To be sure, the failure to know the basis for why a given behavior is right or wrong leads people to hold conflicting opinions.

To Live Consistently with what One Professes

Consider the topic of stealing. Most people readily agree that stealing— taking something that is not one's own without permission from the owner—is morally wrong. Nevertheless, when Edward Snowden, a computer analyst working for the Central Intelligence Agency, copied and leaked classified information in 2013, many people considered his actions heroic. Far from being morally abhorrent, to some, Snowden was a patriot. What made Snowden's actions seem immoral to some and moral to others? Are some people merely inconsistent in their ethical applications, or is there something intrinsic about Snowden's actions that separate his behavior from that of a common thief? The formal study of ethics helps one understand more clearly the basis for why an action is right or wrong, and consequently, helps one to avoid espousing contradictory positions.

To Address the Changing Ethical Climate

In addition, the formal study of ethics helps one to traverse the ethical challenges that confront us as a result of the rapidly changing advances taking place in technology. Genetic engineering and artificial intelligence, for example, are two fields that have burst on to the scene in the past decade and have the potential to greatly affect the lives of everyone. With this progress however, a host of new ethical challenges arise. If someone is killed by a driver-less car, is it still murder? And even though genetic engineering can help many couples who struggle to conceive, where is the ethical line to be drawn for distinguishing the goods that may be achieved through genetic engineering and the evils that were attempted in Hitler's idea of a master race? Thus, the study of ethics aids one in the practice of consistent moral decision-making, provides a solid theological background for understanding why something is morally praiseworthy, and supplies one with the tools needed to live ethically in a changing world. And in this age of globalization, the change seems to be occurring quicker and quicker.

To Affect Our Witness before Others

Lastly, the study of ethics is important because how we live has the potential to affect our witness before others. The apostle Paul commanded Timothy, his son in the faith, to "do the work of the evangelist" (2 Tim. 4:5). As Christians, we are commanded to live in such a way that we are always presenting the gospel to others. How we respond to various situations that might arise within our places of business has the potential to affect our ultimate witness. If, for example, we allow one coworker to sexually harass another without ever attempting to intervene, we might lose credibility about the importance of our faith to our lives before both individuals. On the other hand, if we refuse to participate in unethical behavior, we also make a strong statement before the watching world about what is important and what is right. Not only have we preserved our personal testimony, we have laid the foundation for discussing greater truths with our coworkers.

In his letter to Titus, the apostle Paul makes a similar argument about living the Christian life. He wrote that our behavior has the potential to impact the attitudes of those who oppose Christ (Titus 2:5); it can silence the opponents (2:8), as well as attract them to Christianity (2:10). Paul's argument is not dissimilar from that of Jesus Christ in the Sermon on the Mount. Matthew records Jesus' statement: "In the same way, let your light shine before others, so that they may see your good works and give glory to your Father who is in heaven" (Matt. 5:16, c.f., 1 Pt. 2:12). In other words, our behavior has the power to attract people to Jesus Christ.[5]

What is Ethics?

Not only is ethical reflection and study valuable, it is also important to understand exactly what we mean when we speak of ethics. On a basic level, ethics is simply the study of what is morally right and wrong.[6] Because the present text proposes to approach the subject from a Christian perspective, the definition of ethics might incorporate this aspect. In a classic text on biblical ethics, John Murray writes: "Biblical ethics is concerned with the manner of life and behavior which the Bible requires and which the faith in the Bible produces."[7] In this regard, Murray makes explicit that the Bible serves as the basis of whether or not something is right or wrong.

In his *Doctrine of the Christian Life*, author and theologian John Frame went even further. Frame stated that "Ethics is theology, viewed as a means of determining which human persons, acts, and attitudes receive God's blessing and which do not."[8] More than simply arising from the Bible, Frame equates ethics with theology, making explicit that ethics is part of an overall Christian worldview. In a similar fashion, Carl Henry stated that Christian ethics is a "comprehensive revealed ethic, full-orbed as Christian theology."[9] Frame and Henry rightly capture various aspects of the nature of Christian ethics: namely, that the subject represents a comprehensive worldview that emanates from the Holy Scriptures and that it reflects, consequently, God's assessment concerning what is right and wrong.

Ethics is Theology

Theology, by its very nature, deals with what we think and believe about God and the relationship between God and the universe. Ethics, on the other hand, often refers to how we actually follow Christ in practice. To this end, ethics is synonymous with the Christian life. However, the two concepts should be seen as one topic, and, conversely, to separate them is both unbiblical and unhealthy. What we believe about God—our theology—should establish the foundation for how we live. Consequently, the Christian life—our ethics—provides an invaluable window into and check for our theology.

In a systematic treatment of theology, one usually investigates a common set of doctrines, such as revelation, sin, the church, and eschatology, to name a few. Most treatments divide the study of God into two areas: the nature of God and the works of God, where the works of God include topics like His calling, regeneration, justification, and sanctification. While often discussed separately in theological texts, they collectively form the beginning of the Christian life. In this regard, the formal study of ethics—the Christian life—is part of the doctrine of salvation. To that degree, it is what people really want to talk about when they discuss "applied" theology.

As we previously noted, what we believe should not be separated from how we live.[10] In his *Manual of Theology*, Baptist theologian and author J.L. Dagg beautifully captured the link between what we believe and how we live. He stated:

> The study of religious truth ought to be undertaken and prosecuted from a sense of duty, and with a view to the improvement of the heart. When learned, it ought not to be laid on a shelf, as an object of speculation; but it should be deposited deep in the heart, where its sanctifying power ought to be felt. To study theology, for the purpose of gratifying curiosity, or preparing for a profession, is an abuse and profanation of what ought to be regarded as most holy. To learn things pertaining to God, merely for the sake of amusement, or secular advantage, or

to gratify the mere love of knowledge, is to treat the Most Holy with contempt.[11]

Consequently, some may refer to ethics as an applied or practical theology. But if theology is meant to be lived, then ethics is merely the name we give to this aspect of theology.[12]

Ethics is a Comprehensive Worldview

Ethics also represents a complete worldview.[13] According to author and apologist James Sire, a "worldview is a set of presuppositions which we hold about the basic make-up of our world."[14] These beliefs, according to Sire, may not only be true or false, but also may be held consciously or subconsciously. Either way, they provide the backdrop for our understanding of the way things are.

Consider, for example, the situation surrounding the riots that broke out in Ferguson, Missouri in the summer of 2014 when a white police officer was involved in a fatal shooting of an African American. According to Heather Ann Thompson, a professor at Temple University, the riots were a natural consequence from a lack of police accountability in black communities.[15] Thompson stated that the majority of those rioting had concluded that the police were intentionally racist. During her presidential bid in 2016, Hillary Clinton espoused positions on community policing policies that echoed these same sentiments. At the same time, numerous citizens and politicians made appearances on cable news channels stating that the police were not racist and that incidents like Ferguson were anomalies.[16]

Thus, there were two groups of people who held conflicting opinions about the motives and intentions of police officers in black communities. Because it is impossible for opposite positions to be simultaneously true, one of them must be wrong. But how do we explain these deep-seated beliefs about reality held by proponents in both groups? According to Sire, their conclusions flow from their presuppositions about the world, regardless of whether or not those suppositions are true. If one were raised

> **Exercise 1.2**: Can you think of an example where two groups of people hold opposite views on an issue? What circumstances do you believe led these individuals to draw the conclusions that they did? How does our discussion of worldviews help explain their conclusions? ∎

to believe that the police could not be trusted, then an event like Ferguson is easily interpreted in that light. Conversely, if one were raised to believe that the police are sacrificial participants in the community, then those beliefs are likewise translated into how one interprets the fatal shooting of an African American. So, our presuppositions shape our ethical sentiments and judgments, which means that our worldview produces our ethic.[17]

With regard to worldviews, Christian author and theologian R.C. Sproul records:

> We all have values. We all have some viewpoint about what life is all about. We all have some perspective on the world we live in. We are not all philosophers but we all have a philosophy. Perhaps we haven't thought much about that philosophy, but one thing is certain—we live it out. . . . The theories we live are the ones we really believe.[18]

Everyone makes decisions, and the decisions are made within a system. The term worldview, therefore, refers to our overarching approach to understanding "life's ultimate questions."[19] A person's worldview deals with the intersection of beliefs about the nature of reality, about knowing, about humanity, about God, and about right and wrong. Ronald Nash beautifully highlights these same themes in his book, *Life's Ultimate Questions*.[20] There he notes that our worldview is the means by which we judge and interpret reality. Our worldview reflects, we believe, an accurate view of the world—the way things really are. In a similar way, theology provides the categories and the basis for how the Christian views the world. Christianity has historically espoused a consistent message about what it believes Scripture teaches about these same issues enumerated by Nash.

• **Theology**: God exists. In fact, the Bible does not seek to prove His existence, but rather, it affirms His existence in the opening verses of the Bible: "In the beginning God" (Gen.1:1);

• **Metaphysics**: The Bible teaches that there is both a physical and a spiritual world.

• **Epistemology**: The Bible teaches that one of the ways that we "know" is through divine revelation. Thus, revelation is a valid source of true information.

• **Humanity**: The Bible teaches that humanity is the crown of God's creation. We are created in God's image. And, although the fall has greatly impacted humanity, God's law is still stamped upon our heart.

By addressing these key components, it is clear that Christian theology represents a particular worldview. And because Christian ethics, as we have argued above, is theology, it must therefore also be a worldview. Therefore, one's beliefs about God, nature, knowing, and humanity, naturally affect what one concludes about a number of ethical issues. If one does not believe that God exists, then one would not turn to the Bible to discover an ethic regarding issues of life and death. However, if one believes that God exists and that God has spoken on these issues, then one will search diligently to understand His position.

Exercise 1.3: Actor George Clooney has stated, "I don't believe in heaven and hell. I don't know if I believe in God. All I know is that as an individual, I won't allow this life–the only thing I know to exist–to be wasted." Based on this quote, what can we say about Clooney's worldview? In evaluating this question, discuss each aspect of Clooney's worldview with respect to theology, metaphysics, and epistemology? Can you say anything about Clooney's ethics given this worldview? ■

What is Business Ethics?

Various professional fields now require that new entrants receive formal training in ethics. Consequently, universities have begun offering classes in nursing ethics, engineering ethics, and business ethics. In this regard, we may ask, "What is the connection between ethics in general and ethics in one of these specialized fields?" Or, what is the relationship of ethics to business ethics?

Business Ethics is a Subdivision of Christian Ethics

The field of ethics may be divided in a number of ways. Broadly, for instance, we could delineate secular ethics from Christian ethics. By doing so, we are merely making explicit our source of authority for determining the rightness or wrongness of a particular action. By equating ethics with theology that arises out of the Bible, we have made explicit that in this text we are dealing with Christian ethics. Thus, we stated that ethics deals with the Christian life: what it means to live and act "Christianly."

But the division between secular and non-secular is not the only way to divide the subject. Within Christian ethics, for example, we can further speak of historical ethics, philosophical ethics, or even applied ethics. In historical ethics, for instance, we are seeking to evaluate how the Church has historically evaluated a particular issue, such as divorce. In a treatment of the topic from an historical ethicist's perspective, therefore, we might investigate what various theologians have said on a particular topic, like war. So, we could evaluate war from the perspective of Augustine, or Luther, or Calvin, as well as the contemporary church. Our goal is to determine how the Church's position might have changed and why, as well as to see if it agrees with our exposition of the topic from a Biblical perspective.

In contrast to historical ethics, philosophical ethics ("meta-ethics") deals with broader questions, like: "What is good?"[21] But when most people think of ethics, they are usually thinking of applied ethics ("normative ethics"), which deals with the evaluation of particular ethical issues, such as reproductive technologies, cloning, euthanasia, or capital punishment. Using our earlier division concerning secular and Christian ethics, we investigate these issues from the perspective of Scripture. That is, if ethics is about living Christianly, then applied ethics seeks to ascertain how one who lives Christianly ought to approach these applied topics.

Business Ethics is a Subdivision of Applied Ethics

Most universities that offer classes in these specialized fields, such as nursing, engineering, and business, approach the study as if it were something different than ethics in general. Thus, engineering ethics is investigated as a topic completely separated from business ethics. In this kind of an approach, practitioners are taught that perhaps there is a unique way to "do" engineering ethics or nursing ethics. However, one should view ethics as the broadest field of study, and one should consider engineering and business ethics as individual areas where one can apply ethical training and evaluation. Accordingly, business ethics represents a subcategory of or a special topic within applied ethics. Therefore, we are seeking to examine how one lives Christianly within the business environment.

In the business world, one may encounter ethical situations that seem isolated to a specific area, such as marketing, management, or accounting. In this text, we aim to develop skills that will assist the reader in evaluating these issues from a theologically informed perspective. When I first started college, I had not yet fully settled on a major. As a student in the business department, I was required to take "Calculus for Business." Later, I changed majors and the university would not accept my class in business calculus as sufficient for my new major. I had to take "Calculus for Math and Science Majors." In this new class, I did not learn a new way to do calculus. In both calculus classes, whether for majors or non-majors, we studied mathematical techniques common to any study of calculus: finding the instantaneous rate of change of some variable or the area underneath a curve. Any student from the calculus class for majors who sat in a class of calculus for non-majors would immediately recognize the techniques and tools utilized by the students. They were, in essence, the same class. The real difference was the issues to which calculus was being applied. Science majors, for example, might look at the instantaneous rate of change of the effects of a particular drug in the body, whereas a business major may evaluate the marginal rate of substitution. But, the math tool used to evaluate both questions is the same; it is the derivative.

In the same way, students in business ethics and engineering ethics do not use different techniques or methodologies to evaluate ethical issues than students who take Christian ethics. The only differences should lie in the topics that are evaluated. Why this may seem obvious to most readers, it is not usually approached this way in most universities or ethics texts for specialized fields. To be blunt, most discipline-specific ethics texts do not teach one how to "do" ethics so much as they outline the discipline's professional organization's code as a list of inviolable rights and wrongs. But, that approach is not ethics so much as it is instruction in a particular code of conduct. In this text, therefore, we will first introduce a method for doing ethics, and secondly, we will apply it to issues specific to students in the business world. But if one should ever change fields or look at issues that are not covered in the text, the same methodology should work. This is how you "do" ethics.

Who is the Moral Agent?

The Moral Agent is a Person

In ethics, we are concerned with how to live Christianly. Consequently, we focus our investigation on the behavior of individuals or groups of individuals. That is, moral evaluation is not concerned with inanimate or non-human actors. This does not mean that we are not concerned with ethical treatment of things like dogs or the environment, for we are. Rather, the dog or the environment are not the objects of moral evaluation because they lack other properties that are necessary for moral evaluation.[22]

The Moral Agent is Free

Not only must a moral agent be human, the moral agent must be free to choose. Stated differently, we would not usually consider a person morally guilty for failing to do something that the individual was incapable of doing.[23] Imagine, for example, that I could hypnotize a student in my class, so that unbeknown to the student, I could induce him to steal something from one of his classmates. Because the student was not "free" to act otherwise, we would not consider the person morally guilty.

Thus, if a person in duress is forced to violate some ethical norm, she is not free or morally culpable. Similarly, if a person is mentally-challenged and lacks the capacity for understanding moral options, this person cannot be held responsible for violating particular norms.

On what basis do we evaluate the moral agent?

Having defined the term ethics and the object of moral evaluation–the moral agent–we are now in a position to begin our discussion of adjudicating the morality of the moral agent.

Our main question is this: On what basis do we evaluate the moral agent? Most people immediately conclude that we should judge the morality of another individual based upon how that person acted. Were her actions moral? Did she "do" the right thing? Upon further reflection, however, we realize that this answer is not fully satisfying, because it still leaves too many unanswered questions. For example, Who determines which actions are good or bad? Is the "right thing" to do fixed, or does it change based on the person and the situation?

To be sure, many people seem to approach ethics like they would choose their favorite color; it just one person's opinion, and no single perspective s is necessarily better than another's. When asked to justify why one believes a particular action is good or bad, therefore, one may provide a variety of answers.

• "It just felt right." In contemporary culture, this response is a popular answer for justifying any number of behaviors. For example, a person may defend his homosexual behavior by asserting that God made him this way and it "just feels right." Or, when a loved one is diagnosed with a terminal disease that is accompanied by severe pain, one may justify her participation in taking the person's life by claiming, "It just felt right."

• "It's the law." For some, the right thing may simply mean that an action conforms to some societal standard or law. Thus, one may justify aborting an unwanted child by noting that it does not break the law: it is legal.

• "He said I could." In the same way, one may attempt to defend the morality of one's actions by appealing to directives of another individual, like a spiritual leader. For example, one could argue against the use of contraceptives because the Pope said it was wrong. In all of these examples, the behavior of the individual remains determinative for whether or not a person acted morally. The goodness or badness of a particular behavior, however, changed depending on one's source of moral authority: one's feelings, a written law, or the directives of an individual. From an historical, Christian perspective, this approach has two chief flaws.

First, in all of the aforementioned examples, the source of moral authority is human-centered. Whether the source of moral authority rests in an individual's feelings, a community's laws, or the wishes and directives of a spiritual leader, the authority remains that of a human. And, whenever one's source of ethical authority is human-centered, it is necessarily subjective and changing. In contrast to these human sources of moral authority, ethics from a theologically informed Christian perspective recognizes the Bible alone as its source of moral authority. And though the Bible was written by human authors, the church maintains that its content comes from God and not from the individual (II Tim. 3:16; II Pet. 1:21). The church has historically taught that the moral law of the Bible reflects the character of God, who does not change. Thus, ethics from a theologically informed Christian perspective is objective and unchanging. The "right thing" to do is not determined by the situation or an individual, but rather, it emanates from the revealed will of God found in Scripture.

But having a wrong source of moral authority is not the only reason for the uneasiness associated with the above examples of adjudicating the morality of a moral agent. The second chief flaw with the examples flows from their decision to judge morality on the basis of behavior alone. Christianity has a long history of viewing a moral event from three perspectives: the rightness of one' actions, the rightness of one's heart, and the rightness of one's purpose.[24] For example, in his classic text, *Mere Christianity*, author C.S. Lewis speaks of these same three parts of morality by referring to the relations between man and man, the things inside each man, and the relations between man and the power that made him.[25] Of course, the "relations between man and man" refers to one's actions and how they affect others. When Lewis speaks of "the things inside each man," he is referencing one's disposition or heart. And finally, when Lewis speaks of the "relations between man and his maker," he is indicating the ultimate purpose or goal of one's actions—whom it is meant to please. Thus, proper ethical evaluation necessarily involves all three perspectives, each of which relates directly to the source of moral authority: God's revealed will in Scripture.[26]

The Moral Agent Acted Rightly

Individuals reared in a more conservative atmosphere most likely were taught that having sexual relations before marriage is morally wrong. Thus, how would you anticipate people from this group responding if I posed the questions, "Is sex before marriage good or bad (meaning morally right or wrong)?" With our penchant for focusing on one's actions for determining the morality of an event, we might quickly respond that the behavior is morally bad. However, this simple exercise readily shows how a focus on behavior alone can lead to a wrong conclusion. That is, if a person chooses to engage in sexual relations before marriage, then we might conclude that the person has acted immorally. However, if the individual were raped, then few would consider her to have acted badly. To be sure, this example allows us to see the moral event from various vantage points.

First, we might say that the person who is raped was not "free" to do otherwise. You may recall that a moral agent must be both a person and free to choose. Being violated against one's will assures that one was not free.

Secondly, focusing on the act alone for making a moral decision leaves us frustrated and confused on how to explain how the rape victim in the example above is not morally culpable for having had pre-marital sex, whereas the person who engages in consensual pre-marital sex is morally culpable for having pre-marital sex. However, evaluating the event through the prism of the three parts of morality helps us better to explain these differences. Let us continue this example by looking at the other parts.

The Moral Agent Acted from a Right Heart

With regard to the action, we might appeal to our source of moral authority—Scripture—and say that consensual sexual relations before marriage are wrong (Deut 22:25 - 27). In addition, we could say something about the heart or disposition of one who willingly engages in premarital sexual relations. If one has been taught that it is wrong, then this behavior would appear to emanate from a heart that is selfish, rather than one that is focused on love for others.

The Moral Agent Acted for a Right Purpose

Lastly, we could also say something about the purpose or goal of the couple who engages in consensual sexual relations before marriage. It would appear that each one is driven by the desire to please self rather than please God. For these reasons, we can see how we might rightly conclude that sexual relations before marriage for a couple willingly engaging in sexual relations is morally wrong. Each acted wrongly according to the source of moral authority; each acted from a selfish heart; and, lastly, each sought his/her own glory rather than that of his/her maker, to use Lewis' term.

In the following chapters, we will explore further this tri-perspectival framework for evaluating a moral event. We will explore in greater detail each perspective—the action, the heart, and the purpose—as well as practice applying it in various situations. This dual purpose of understanding the theological/philosophical foundation and the practical application provide the basis for how the text will proceed.

Summary

At the most basic level, ethics is living and acting Christianly. By adding the adverb "Christianly," we make clear that the "living" and the "acting" spring from a life that is informed by the biblical Scriptures and has been empowered to live and to act through the indwelling Holy Spirit. In addition, ethics represents a full-orbed worldview. What one thinks about the nature of God, knowing, and reality necessarily affects one's beliefs about right and wrong. An individual that is theologically informed from a Christian perspective will undoubtedly arrive at moral conclusions that differ from those who operate from a secular mindset. To be sure, the application of ethics in the business arena will look vastly different for these two worldviews.

The study of business ethics, as we have defined it, will most certainly include numerous benefits, such as providing a basis for understanding why an action is right or wrong, as well as assisting one to live a more consistently moral life. Finally, we note that in our striving to live ethically in the business world not only requires that we do the right thing (as defined by our source of moral authority), but we must also act from a right heart and for a right purpose.

Chapter 2:
Right Conduct in Business Ethics

Over the past ten years, few topics have gripped our nation more than the subject of illegal immigration. While it is impossible to know exactly how many people are entering the country illegally, the US Border Patrol reported approximately 688,375 border apprehensions between October 2018 and July 2019. In May of 2019 alone, there were more than 120,000 individuals arrested for crossing the southern border between United States and Mexico.

To some degree, these large numbers represent a national security issue. With the growing number of people crossing the border, border resources are stretched thin. With mass migration of refugees particularly from areas inundated with religious and political violence, the United States is seeing more entrants from these areas. US intelligence officials reported that two al-Qaeda linked refugees were living in Bowling Green, Kentucky, having arrived as admitted members for resettlement.

But the immigration issue is not just a security issue, it also represents an important topic for business ethics. How are Christian business owners supposed to think about this issue? Consider how a Christian might respond to a member of the church who is living in the United States illegally and working in a local industry. How are Christians to react?

Is it as simple as claiming that those entering the country and staying illegally are breaking the law? Is the primary argument from a Christian perspective to appeal to God's moral standard about submitting to those in authority? Does Paul's argument in Romans 13 settle the issue for business owners? Would your answer change if you knew that the individual had left his country of origin because of famine, starvation, or violence? Would your answer change if you knew the individual was sending money home to the foreign country where his wife and three young children live? How does the illegal immigrant simultaneously balance the call to obey the laws of government in Romans 13 and Paul's admonition to provide for the members of his household (1 Tim. 5:8)? How does the Believer balance his respect for government and laws with his pro-life position? These are not easy questions. In this chapter, we want to explore the first portion of the three parts of morality by focusing on topic of right conduct.

Exercise 2.1: From the brief introduction about illegal immigration, state a moral question worthy of investigation. Be sure to use moral language, such as "morally permissible" or "morally obligated." ∎

In the previous chapter, we discussed various important questions related to doing business ethics from a Christian perspective. In our exploration of the nature of ethics, we showed that Christian ethics, informed by Scripture, is a worldview. As a worldview, Christian ethics makes metaphysical and epistemological claims – namely, that God exists and that God speaks. While these two terms seem philosophical and academic in nature with little applicability in the real world, they ultimately form the basis for our conclusions regarding the morality of a moral event, such as the issue of illegal immigration described above.

Springs from God's Existence

Surely, one of the greatest crises facing humanity today is epistemological in nature. Namely, how do we know and teach what we claim to know and teach? In his book, *He Is There and He Is Not Silent*, author and apologist Francis Schaeffer confronted this very question. [1] In the title alone, the author makes two bold worldview claims: namely, that God exists and that God speaks. Of first importance for our present discussion, Schaeffer asserts that God exists, or to use his words, "God is There." This truth about God's existence undergirds the theological and metaphysical portion of our worldview categories. In short, we are arguing that "reality" includes both a physical and spiritual world. By definition, nothing is higher or more ultimate than God. He is the source of moral authority.

The Implications for an Atheistic Worldview

Certainly we live in a time where many people might doubt the existence of a God. Perhaps you have encountered the writings and philosophies of people like Richard Dawkins or Stephen Hawking. Both of these individuals have sought to use their standing in the scientific community to make bold claims about the non-existence of God. Atheists' arguments about God's non-existence carry ethical implications. If there is no God, then their source of moral authority must be human-centered. And, if it is humanly centered, then it must be changing and relative.

The Implications for an Agnostic Worldview

In the same way, others may not be as certain as Dawkins and Hawking. They do not deny the existence of God; rather, they are simply uncertain of whether or not God exists. Nevertheless, their lack of clear commitment to God's existence carries ethical ramifications. Because the agnostic cannot be certain that "God is there," he looks to a human-centered source for his moral decisions. This human source, of course, could include any number of possible choices, such as himself, humanly constructed moral codes, or even spiritual leaders. Whatever the source, we can be assured it is relative and changing.

The Implications for a Christian Worldview

The Christian worldview, however, flowing from the Bible asserts with confidence that God is in fact present. Like the metaphysical claims of the atheist and the agnostic, the Christian worldview has moral implications. Namely, if God exists, then he defines our ethical system, and those ethical norms are absolute and unchanging because they are based upon a God who is unchanging. But Schaeffer asserted more than God's existence. He also claimed that God is not silent.

Springs from God's Revelation

If we believe there is a God but he is silent, then our worldview is still like that of the atheist and agnostic. It is as if we live in a box, and God is outside the box. He does not affect what takes place inside the box, and we cannot access his mind or his will. However, if God is not silent, then everything changes. This is where the Christian theory of knowledge–epistemology–is so important. We believe that God has spoken.

What do we mean when we say that God's speaking forms part of the Christian's epistemology? Recall that epistemology refers to a theory of knowledge. One's epistemology attempts to answer questions about truth claims. Since the 1500s, many philosophers have developed epistemologies specifically to address religious truth claims. Rene Descartes, John Locke, and Immanuel Kant, for example, represent three major epistemological camps– camps in which many individuals in contemporary society, interestingly, align themselves.

• Rene Descartes represented the epistemological school known as rationalism. According to rationalists, the ultimate source of knowledge is human reason.

• In contrast to rationalists, John Locke and David Hume espoused a theory of knowledge known as empiricism, which claims that knowledge is associated with sense experience. It is associated with empirical evidence that arises out of scientific experience. Thus, we can make truth claims about the density of gold or the boiling temperature of water based upon scientific experiments.

• Immanuel Kant is associated with the philosophical camp known as idealism, which stressed the primacy of ideas or the spiritual in one's interpretation of experience.[2] To some degree, Kant agreed with the empiricists – that we could have some knowledge of this world because we have sensory input and we can empirically test it. Nevertheless, Kant considered empiricism a serious attack upon human dignity. If

Empiricism were the only theory of knowledge, Kant argued, then humanity is nothing more than a complex animal that adds and compares empirical sensations. Thus, Kant stressed a knowledge that was not derivable from sense experience alone. In essence, Kant argued that true knowledge is a joint product of rational innate forms and sense experience. Like rationalists, Kant claimed that reason supplied forms, and like the empiricists, Kant asserted that sense experience supplied the content.

Why is this discussion of epistemology important? Kant made, perhaps, the most significant contribution to our discussion of epistemology. Basically, Kant denied the possibility of objective knowledge of anything metaphysical, or what he called *noumenal*. We can have some knowledge of the physical world, what he called *phenomenal* reality, because we have sensory input and we can empirically test and know it. But Kant would not accept revelation as a source for knowledge. Rather, as the title of one of his major works testifies, he insisted on religion only "within the bounds of reason." In Kant and the Enlightenment in general, reason reigned supreme, and reason will not place itself under a supposed revelation from God. Rather, reason examines revelation and sees many ideas and statements it cannot accept – miracles and such. These things are not part of our everyday experience, and so cannot be accepted by reason.

In short, Kant neither denied the existence of God nor the spiritual world. To the contrary, Kant believed in these things. In his theory of knowledge, however, Kant contended that we cannot "know" anything about God nor the spiritual world. God may be there and God may speak, but we cannot know it. In other words, revelation is not a valid source of knowledge. But if we operate from a Christian worldview, then we must reject Kant's critique. We believe that God does speak and that we are capable of receiving this revelation. This epistemological declaration about revelation separates Christian ethics from secular ethics. These two truths – that God exists and God speaks – provide us the basis for all ethical evaluation. The Christian epistemology does not reject the validity of reason or experience. To be sure, we know some things by reason, such as the law of non-contradiction. Similarly, we know some things by experience, such as fire is hot and should not be touched. The primary weakness of secular epistemologies is not in what they affirm, but rather, in what they deny.[3] They reject revelation as a valid source of knowing. But we are not surprised by this rejection. If secularists reject the existence of God, then logically, they must likewise deny that God speaks.

Ultimately, our opinions about the ethical behavior of others are just that – our opinions. But if God exists and he has spoken about a particular issue, then his opinion is of greatest importance. We are

> **Exercise 2.2**: In your own words, write what is meant by the phrases "Christian metaphysic" and "Christian epistemology." ∎

arguing in this text that God indeed has spoken to issues like those addressed in the example about illegal immigration. From a Christian

> **Exercise 2.3**: What two components of a Christian worldview are most important for establishing a foundation for Christian ethics? Why? ∎

worldview, God is the basis of truth, because he is truth (Isa. 65:16) and his words are true (II Sam. 7:28). Consequently, all ethical evaluation begins with examining what God has said. In theological terms, we refer to God's speaking as revelation. Often discussions of God's revelation are divided into two broad categories based upon the breadth of the audience: general revelation, which refers to God's disclosure to everyone and special revelation, which refers to God's disclosure to specific individuals at specific times. Regardless of the method of revelation, the content is the same. When God speaks, he unveils both himself and his will.[4]

God Reveals Himself

Regardless of the source of revelation (i.e., Scripture, nature, history, persons, etc.,), God reveals himself.[5] Through a multitude of sources, therefore, God has chosen to make himself known.[6]

In Nature

For example, the natural world has long been recognized as a valid source through which God can speak. The Psalmist records: "The heavens declare the glory of God, and the sky above proclaims his handiwork. Day to day pours out speech, and night to night reveals knowledge" (Ps 19:1 -2). In Paul's first missionary journey, the author of Acts records that he miraculously healed a man who was crippled in the,city of Lystra. As a result of the healing, some of the people began to conclude that Paul and Barnabas were gods, like Jupiter and Mercury.

> But when the apostles Barnabas and Paul heard it, they tore their garments and rushed out into the crowd, crying out, "Men, why are you doing these things? We also are men, of like nature with you, and we bring you good news that you should turn from these vain things to a living God, who made the heaven and the earth and the sea and all that is in them. In the past generations he allowed all the nations to walk in their own ways. Yet, he did not leave himself without witness, for he did good by giving you rains from heaven and fruitful seasons, satisfying your hearts with food and gladness." (Acts 14:14 - 17)

Paul implored the people to turn from polytheism to the one true and "living God" (14:15). Moreover, Paul identified this living God with the Creator of the heavens and the earth (14:16). In the end, Paul argues that the people of Lystra can know this God, because God "did not leave himself without witness" (14:17). God had revealed himself through his natural providence: God sent rain for their crops and provided food.

In a similar passage, the author of Acts records Paul's message to the people of Athens while standing in the midst of the Areopagus.

After acknowledging their ignorance of the one true God by having an altar to "an unknown god," Paul introduced them to the Creator, "who made the world and everything in it" (17:24). In this passage, however, Paul describes more extensively God's creative involvement: "[God] himself gives to all mankind life and breath and everything. And he made from one man every nation of mankind to live on all the face of the earth, having determined allotted periods and the boundaries of their dwelling place" (17:25-26). Most importantly from Paul's message, however, is Paul's explanation for God's creation: that humanity should "seek" God and "find him" (17:28). Like his sermon in Lystra, Paul insists that God has made himself known through his providential goodness in the created order, and equally important, that God should be sought.

In his letter to the church at Rome, Paul describes in detail the universal breadth of God's self-manifestation (Rom. 1:18 - 32).

• He teaches that the revelation is clear: "is plain to them" (1:19).

• He teaches that the revelation is "about God" and from God: "God has shown it to them" (1:19).

• He teaches that the revelation is mediated through the created universe: "the creation of the world in the things that have been made" (1:20).

• He teaches that rejection of God's revelation carries serious moral consequences: "wrath of God is revealed . . . against unrighteousness . . . so they are without excuse . . . and those who practice such things deserve to die" (1:18; 20; 32). To make the point explicit, God is making himself known in each of these examples as opposed to simply providing information about soteriology. And, to go further, Paul witnesses this connection between God's revelation in nature and revelation of God in his Scriptures. Therefore, the Holy Scriptures are replete with examples of God making himself known via nature. We see it in the Psalms, in the narrative history of the church in Acts, and in the theological letters of Paul.

In Persons

God has not only chosen to make himself known through the natural order, but he also has chosen to reveal himself through persons. This fact should not surprise us, since both the natural world and humanity itself are creations of God. Perhaps the most important aspect of God's creation of humanity is His choice to create men and women in his own image: "Then God said, 'Let us make man in our image, after our likeness. And let them have dominion over the fish of the sea and over the birds of the heavens and over the livestock and over all the earth and over every creeping thing that creeps on the earth'" (Gen. 1:26). The creation narrative in Genesis conveys God's sovereignty over everything. God merely spoke, and things came into existence (1:3, 6-7, 9, 11, 14-15, 20-21, and 24). God named things (1:5, 8, and 10). Lastly, God morally evaluated his creation as "good" and "very good" (1:4, 9, 12, 18, 21, 25, and 31).[7]

Being created in God's image suggests that God made a creature similar to himself. Men and women share the likeness of their creator. Since the author of Genesis does not catalog the many ways that humanity shares in God's likeness, then neither will we.[8] Nevertheless, we assume that it at least refers to God creating humanity as a moral creature and charged with the command to "be fruitful . . . subdue . . . and have dominion" (1:28). As an image bearer, God charged humanity to be like him. Just as God created, ordered, and named, so also was humanity to practice these things.[9] In this sense, humans do not merely possess the image of God; rather, humans are the image of God (c.f. I Cor. 11:7). By our creation in God's image, we (can) manifest aspects of who God is (although in an imperfect way).

In Scripture

Finally, God has also chosen to make himself known through the written Word: the Scriptures. If humanity were not affected by sin, then general revelation would be sufficient for us to know God. But humanity in a fallen state suppresses the truth (Rom. 1:18). In short, sin has blinded us so that God's revelation of himself through nature therefore, must be supplemented by written and spoken word.[10]

Because revelation in nature, persons, and Scripture has the same author, the content of the revelation is consistent. The clearest expression of this revelation is Jesus, who said, "Whoever has seen me has seen the Father" (Jn.14:9). But the church has historically maintained that the written word–Scripture–is the primary source for knowing and under-standing God. The Bible, like God's revelation in nature, affirms God's role in creation (Gen. 1 - 2; John 1:3; Eph. 3:9;, Col.1:16, Rev.4:11). Moreover, Scripture affirms that God continues to actively participate in this world through his providential care–sustaining life (Ps. 36:6-9; 104:10-30; Acts 14:17; Heb. 1:3) and directing all things to his ultimate purposes for them (Gen. 50:20; Acts 2:23, Rom. 8:28, Ps 135:5-7).

As the creator and sustainer of the universe, we would expect God to be greater and more powerful than any other force. We can summarize this greatness of God with the term infinite. God is infinite in power (i.e., omnipotent), infinite in space (i.e., omnipresent), infinite in time (i.e., eternal) (Ps. 90:1 - 2), infinite in knowledge (i.e, omniscient) (Ps 139:1 - 12; Rom. 11:33 - 36; Heb. 4:13), and God is infinite in all of his attributes, such as love, holiness, mercy and wrath (Ps 36:5-6).

Even the narrative stories found in the Bible reveal who God is. Consider broadly some of the stories found in the Pentateuch, the first five books of the Bible.[11] First, we see that God is sovereign. There is nothing that lies outside his control. God's manifested his sovereignty several times throughout the Pentateuch in stories about creation, God's deliverance of Israel from Egypt, and even in God's gift of the land of Promise. As Creator, God is the owner of all lands and can give them to whomever He desires. In Deuteronomy, for example, He designated particular properties to the Edomites (Deut. 2:5), the Moabites (Deut. 2:9), and the Ammonites (Deut. 2:19) in much the same way that He designated the Garden for Adam and Eve (Gen. 2:8; c.f. Gen. 3:23–24). Consequently, the reader is not surprised by God's decision to give land previously designated for Israel to Israel (Gen. 15:16–21). In short, it is his land, and he can give it to whomever he pleases.

Secondly, the reader continues to see the graciousness of God in the book of Deuteronomy. In fact, God's graciousness was tied to his decision to give land to Israel, whom Moses often depicts in language that demonstrates her unworthiness. But God, in his grace and kindness, granted Israel the privilege of living and "resting" in the land as long as she maintained the covenant.

Finally, no book in the Pentateuch reflects the covenant faithfulness of God more than the book of Deuteronomy. From the opening pages of the book, Moses recounts the history of God's relationship with Israel. Everything that God promised Abraham—land, a name, posterity, and blessing—comes into stark focus through the pages of Deuteronomy and the sermons of Moses. Certainly, these promises encountered numerous threats throughout Israel's history—slavery in Egypt and wandering in the desert—but God remembered his covenant with Abraham. God is sovereign, gracious, and faithful.[12]

God Reveals His Will

Through nature, other persons, and through the written Word, we see how God has labored to make himself known. He desperately desires that we know him intimately. We see this kind of relationship in Genesis characterized by Adam and Eve walking in the garden with their Creator—a relationship not yet affected by the intrusion of sin. Through the various modes of revelation, however, God has done more than reveal himself; he has also endeavored to make known his will. That is, God not only desires that we come to know him, but he also longs for us to "walk" or "live" in a certain way. The two primary ways that God's revelation of his will intersects with Christian ethics is through his creation of humanity after his own image and through his revelation in Scripture.

In Human Conscience

We stated earlier that being created in God's image suggests that God made a creature similar to himself. Men and women share the likeness of their creator. While the Bible does not define for us the precise content of the original image, it has historically been associated with at least humanity's rational and moral aptitudes.[13] Consequently, humanity was endowed with an innate concern for morality and truth. Carl Henry wrote with point: "Man possessed an ability to discern the will of God concerning all the duties required of him. He had a disposition to perform those duties. And he was eager to translate that disposition into ready compliance and performance."[14] Accordingly, Adam and Eve were not only capable of moral choice, but equally were they culpable for their choices. Reformed theologian, Albert Wolters, drives home this point when he writes:

> Even without God's explicit verbal positivization of the creational norms . . . people have an intuitive sense of normative standards for conduct. One word for that intuitive attunement to creational normativity is conscience. . . . This does not refer to some innate virtue of 'natural man,' unaffected by sin, but to the finger of the sovereign Creator engraving reminders of his norms upon human sensibilities even in the midst of apostasy.[15]

Indeed, Paul affirms that by creation in the image of God one has access to the moral standards of God. This point was the basis of his argument to the church at Rome. He stated: "For all who have sinned . . . will perish" (Rom. 2:12). Further, he says that this judgment is sure whether one is a Gentile or a Jew. Both have transgressed God's holy law. However, one may object that the Gentiles did not have access to the law like the Jews. Paul argues that while the Gentiles did not have the law written on stone tablets (Ex. 24:12), they nevertheless had the law stamped upon their heart, merely as a result of being created in God's image.

> For when Gentiles, who do not have the law, by nature do what the law requires, they are a law to themselves, even though they do not have the law. They show that the work of the law is written on their hearts, while their conscience also bear witness, and their conflicting thoughts accuse or even excuse them (Rom. 2:14-15).

What God has written on the heart finds a response in man's conscience. Hence, conscience becomes the vehicle for communicating moral content. The accusers of the woman caught in adultery were convicted of their own sin (John 8:9). In contrast, Paul says that his conscience bears testimony that he acted godly (II Cor. 1:12). Because it communicates ethical knowledge, Scripture exhorts us to have "good conscience" (Acts 23:1; 1 Tim. 1:5, 19; 1 Pet. 3:21) and a "clear conscience" (Acts 24:16; I Tim. 3:9). Nevertheless, the conscience can also be perverted. Paul speaks of false teachers "whose consciences are seared" (1 Tim. 4:2). Dave Jones rightly concludes, "It is clear that the conscience is a tool God uses to regulate (if not to reveal) his moral standards to all of mankind.[16]

In Scripture

Although God uses our conscience to speak to us, our conscience is not the final authority for determining our Christian moral duty. To the contrary, Scripture is the locus of God's revelation. The Westminster Shorter Catechism asks, "What rule hath God given to direct us how we may glorify and enjoy him?" The answer: "The Word of God, which is contained in the Scriptures of the Old and New Testaments, is the only rule to direct us how we may glorify and enjoy him." While God does "speak" through things created (nature and persons), God also speaks through the written Word: Scripture.

We showed earlier that readers encounter God in Scripture. In addition, readers are confronted with moral standards of God. Paul writes, "All Scripture is breathed out by God and profitable for teaching, for reproof, for correction, and for training in righteousness that the man of God may be complete, equipped for every good work" (2 Tim. 3:16-17). All Scripture owes its origin to the divine breath of God. To be sure, because the words are from God, they are "profitable." Paul notes some of the areas where Scripture is profitable, such as teaching truth about Christ, reproof for errors in doctrine, correction toward the right path, and lastly, for training in righteousness. Although every aspect of obedience has a moral component, "training in righteousness" points to the normative character of God's moral law. In short, the prophet Micah nicely summarizes this point: "He has told you, O man, what is good; and what does the Lord

> **Exercise 2.4**: If God has spoken and made his will known, how might we apply it to the illegal immigration case? What passages or moral principles might apply in this example? ∎

require of you but to do justice, and to love kindness, and to walk humbly with your God" (Micah 6:8).

Springs from Humanity's Moral Duty to God's Revelation

All that we have said thus far is that God has spoken, and that in his speech, he has told us something about himself and his will for us. But God did not reveal himself merely to satisfy our curiosities, but rather, he revealed himself that we might know him and develop the type of obedient, intimate relationship for which he created us (Deut. 29:20, II Tim. 3:15-17). Stated differently, God's revelation carries with it a duty to obey. God's revelation, therefore, is both indicative and imperative.[17] For example, the Psalmist explains that God's revelation declares his glory. It is indicative. "The heavens declare the glory of God" (Ps. 19:1). Similarly, Paul declares that this same creation reveals God's nature: "For his invisible attributes, namely, his eternal power and divine nature, have been clearly perceived, ever since the creation of the world" (Rom.1:20). But this same revelation in Psalms and Romans carries with it a divine imperative: "Let the words of my mouth and the meditation of my heart be acceptable in your sight, O Lord my rock and my redeemer" (Ps. 19:14). Paul similarly shows the imperative nature of God's revelation when he writes that the God is pouring out his wrath on those who did not honor him. His revelation demands a response.

In ethical discourse, this approach to ethics based on a "duty" to obey is called deontological. The term deontological is derived from the Greek word *deon*, which means duty or obligation. A deontological ethics, therefore, is a duty-based ethics.[18] This approach to ethics stands in stark contrast to various ethical theories, but most often it is pitted against utilitarianism (or consequentialism), which focuses moral evaluation of an act on the consequences that result.

By way of example, consider a study by the United States Public Health Service between 1932 and 1972.[19] The Health Service wanted to understand better the natural history and progression of syphilis, a sexually transmitted disease that can lead to death. They studied syphilis in order to better diagnose and treat the ailment. Most would consider this purpose as good and positive. The manner in which the Public Health Service conducted the study, however, does not appear equally good or positive.

In order to conduct the study, the Public Health Service collaborated with Tuskegee University to enroll African-American sharecroppers from Macon County, Alabama. Later portions of the study included 127 black medical students. According to the Center of Disease Control and Prevention, nearly two-thirds of the initial participants in the study had previously contracted syphilis.[20] Although participants were originally told that the study would last for six months, it actually continued for forty years. Most important for our discussion, none of the participants were treated for their syphilis, even though they had been led to believe that they were being treated. Consequently, those who had syphilis experienced the horrible pain and discomfort that accompanies the disease, and eventually they died.

If we were to evaluate this moral event from a consequentialist perspective, we might conclude that it was ethically good. That is, because in the "end," we learned something good that will help others, then the act of lying to the participants and not treating their disease was ethically good. In utilitarian language, it resulted in the greatest good for the greatest number of people, because now, thousands of people have benefited from the research that resulted from the study.

In contrast to the utilitarian approach to ethics, a deontological ethic does not focus on the ends for determining the goodness or badness of a moral event, but rather, concentrates its evaluation of the moral agent on the morality of the act itself. Did the moral agent perform an action that itself was morally good? From this perspective, one might say that it is never right to withhold life-saving medical treatment for the mere purpose of medical advancement. One has a moral "duty" to preserve innocent human lives. Thus, a deontologist would conclude that the Tuskegee syphilis study was immoral because the actors did not fulfill their moral duty.

While deontological ethics is duty-based, it may appear in ethical reasoning in a number of varieties, such as human rights, natural law, Kantian, principled monism, or divine command to name a few. For example, a principled monist would argue that a moral agent has a duty to one principle–one law if you will.[21] In his *Situation Ethics*, for example, Joseph Fletcher argued that the supreme moral duty was love. In fact, it was the only command to which the moral agent was ethically bound.[22]

German philosopher Immanuel Kant likewise promoted a deontological ethic. Kant proposed a "categorical imperative," which served as a guiding principle for all actions. He wrote: "A categorical imperative would be one which represented an action as objectively necessary in itself apart from its relation to a further end."[23] Kant described one formulation of his principle like this: "Act as if the maxim of thy action were to become by thy will a Universal Law of Nature."[24] By universalizing his principle, Kant argued that it ought to motivate the action of any moral agent in an ethical situation. Thus, the moral rightness of a moral agent is based upon the agent's duty to act a certain way.

Thus, just because an ethic is deontological does not mean that it is a Christian ethic. What is most important in a deontological ethic, therefore, is the content and source of the duty. The specific variety of deontology most appropriate for our study is divine command theory. A divine command ethic asserts that morality finds its basis in God. God commands that which is good and God forbids that which is evil.[25] Again, Carl Henry summarizes this doctrine best when he writes:

> Hebrew-Christian ethics centers in Divine revelation of the statutes, commandments, and precepts of the Living God. Its whole orientation of the moral life may be summarized by what the Holy Lord commands and what he forbids: what accords with his edicts is right, what opposes his holy will is wicked.[26]

Duty to Obey God's Moral Standards

In the Christian Scriptures, which we previously identified as our primary and authoritative source for God's revelation, we have access to God's moral standards. While these standards may come in the form of imperatives, like the Ten Commandments, they may also appear in other genres as well. All of Scripture is inspired and is revelation from God. Consequently, whether the revelation is history, poetry, song, parable, apocalyptic, or simple narrative, it remains a significant source for ethics. While it is perhaps easiest to recognize what pleases God in an imperative, all forms of literature equally convey God's moral standards. Consider, for example, God's revealed moral standards with regard to marital faithfulness. In the seventh commandment's prohibition against adultery, God communicates that faithfulness is morally praise worthy and infidelity is evil. But God communicates the same truth in the prophetic book of Hosea, as well as the historical narrative about David and Bathsheba, and in the wisdom literature of Proverbs (e.g. Prov. 5:15). Regardless of the genre of biblical literature, if the narrative reflects God's approval or triggers his wrath, we have a duty to act accordingly. In this sense, the conduct that God approves, even if revealed in historical narrative rather than an imperative, remains nevertheless a divine command.

Some critics of divine command theory suppose that Plato's Euthyphro dilemma renders it dead. In Plato's *Euthyphro*, the student asks, "Is an act pious because the gods command it or do the gods command it because it is pious?"[27] This question seems to have only two options, neither of which seem good to proponents of divine command theory. If one argues that acts are right and good because God commands them, then God's commands appear arbitrary. If on the other hand, God commands what he does because it is right, then morality does not depend on God's commands after all. God merely recognizes that which is moral.[28]

Christian writers have historically responded to the Euthyphro dilemma by noting that a third option exists. The law which God commands is good and right because it reflects and reveals the character of God, which is moral and upright.[29] Geisler echoes this point when he writes, "[T]he ethical imperatives that God gives are in accord with his unchangeable moral character."[30] Perhaps the clearest expression of the historic Christian position comes from the pen of Carl Henry. He writes:

> In stipulating the moral law, the Creator-God lay under no necessity other than to form it according to his own pleasure, and hence in conformity with his real character and purpose. The will of God so reveals his character that the man who conforms to his commandments will exhibit the image of God in his life.

The Hebrew-Christian knowledge of God is a knowledge of the Righteous One.[31]

The moral standards, therefore, are the manifested will of God. God commands us to "not commit adultery" (Ex. 20:14) because God himself is faithful. God commands us not to "bear false witness" (Ex. 20:16), because God is truth and "cannot tell a lie" (Heb. 6:18). Ultimately, God commands us to "be holy" (Lev. 11:45) because he himself is holy. God commands that which is in accordance with his character, and in the commands, we catch a glimpse of the character of God.

> **Exercise 2.5**: A good summary of God's moral standards are found in the Ten Commandments. Which one of the Ten Commandments might best apply to the question of whether Christians are morally permitted to deny using their "artistic" skills (e.g. baker, florist, photographer, etc.) for celebrating events that they believe are immoral? ∎

Duty to Imitate God

Therefore, when we keep God's commands, we are actually imitating God. Among God's many attributes, he is a moral being. In keeping with his moral nature, God judges rightly and he exhibits righteousness in all that he does. Previously, we noted that God reveals himself in persons. Being created in God's image suggests that God made a creature similar to himself. We too are moral beings. And just as he created and filled, we too receive this charge from God: "be fruitful . . . subdue . . . and have dominion" (1:28). As an image bearer, God charged humanity to be like him. Just as God created, ordered, and named, so also was humanity to practice these things.[32] Long-time professor of theology at Westminster Seminary, John Murray aptly wrote:

In the last analysis, why must we behave in one way and not in another? . . . The ultimate standard of right is the character or nature of God. The basis of ethics is that God is what he is, and we must be conformed to what he is in holiness, righteousness, truth, goodness, and love. . . . God made man in his own image and after his likeness. Man must, therefore, be like God.[33]

Therefore, a significant way in which we can glorify God is imitation. Hence, we are not surprised that God's Word instructs the people of God to "be imitators of God" (Eph. 5:1) or to be holy as he is holy (Lev. 11:45; 1 Pet. 1:16). In other places, we are commanded to "be merciful even as your Father is merciful" (Luke 6:36) and "perfect as your heavenly Father is perfect (Matt. 5:48).Consequently, we have a duty not only to obey God's moral standards, which reflects and reveals his character, but we also have a moral duty to imitate God. Such imitation brings him glory.[34]

> **Exercise 2.6**: In the previous question we looked at principles and commands from God's Word that might apply to the illegal immigration situation. Are there aspects of God's character that we have a duty to imitate that might inform how judge the morality of the moral agent in the illegal immigration case? ∎

Summary

In this chapter, we have addressed one of the three major parts of morality: right conduct. We have argued that right conduct, according to a Christian worldview, springs from a biblical metaphysic and biblical epistemology: namely, from the conviction that God exists and that God has spoken. Because God exists and has spoken, his opinion in matters of right and wrong are what is most important. Moreover, because right conduct emanates from God, it is normative and unchanging.

As a result of God's decision to speak, he revealed both himself and his will. This revelation is available in various modes, such as nature, persons, and Scripture. But because each source has the same author, its content is unchanged. Nevertheless, Scripture is the primary timeless source of moral revelation. Regardless of the source, we have a moral duty to obey this revelation.

Chapter 3:
Right Heart in Business Ethics

Union membership is a controversial topic from both a political and business perspective. Most unions strive to improve work conditions, raise wages for its members, and prevent injustice in the workplace. By uniting the voices of the workers into one, unions can increase pressure on management to accepting the majority of its proposals. Consequently, union workers typically receive better benefits and higher wages than non-union employees.

Despite these benefits, overall union membership has decreased significantly over the past thirty years. Only 10.7% of salaried workers belong to a union in the U.S. today, which is half of what it used to be in 1983. The main reason for this drop in membership is due to the shift in jobs from manufacturing to service as a result of improved technology.[1]

Union membership, however, is not limited by any means to the manufacturing industry. Employees of practically every industry have union members, such as education, health services, transportation, broadcasting, and television show writers. And even though overall union membership has decreased in recent years, unions continue to affect significant numbers of people in various careers and across multiple social strata.[2]

Consequently, Christians in the marketplace might question whether or not they are morally permitted to join unions. To be sure, if all of life is lived *coram deo*, it is incumbent upon Christians to consider what God's Word might say about such activities. In the previous chapter, we argued that Christians have a moral duty to God's moral standards and to imitate God's character. But union membership seems to be a difficult question since the Bible does not seem to address it directly. In this kind of situation, how might one go about discerning God's moral standards?

Would my position on joining a union change based on the types of activities and issues the union supported with members' dues? Does Paul's admonition about being yoked with unbelievers apply to this situation (2 Cor. 6:14)? How does God's command against coveting and exhortation toward contentment influence my understanding of a Christian's response to union membership?

In this chapter, we move from our discussion of right conduct to right heart – considering what kind of person we ought to be. That is, in this chapter we want to explore who we are more than what we do. To be sure, who we are is intricately related to how we live. To that end, perhaps we might better answer the question about union membership by asking "What kind of person should I be?" Stated differently, what kind of activities should I pursue so that I might become one who is characterized as content in all things?

> **Exercise 3.1**: From the introductory story, list three characteristics of a moral agent who is being formed into the image of Jesus Christ. ∎

In this chapter, we want to bring together two previously introduced concepts: the three parts of morality and the issue of ethics as theology. First, with regard to the three parts of morality, we noted in the introduction that morality has three necessary components: right conduct, right heart, and right purpose. In the previous chapter, we focused our discussion of the individual's moral duty to the revealed will of God on right conduct: the moral agent must act or behave himself in a manner consistent with God's moral standards. In this chapter, we want to extend that conversation to discussing the second component of the moral event: a right heart. We noted that doing the right action from a wrong heart still results in a negative evaluation of the moral agent; it is still unethical.

Our current focus on the heart of the moral agent is deeply connected with a second major concept that we presented in the introduction: ethics is theology or applied theology. As theology, ethics is concerned with what we think about God and how that thinking is translated into living. Within our discussion of ethics as theology, we equated ethics with the Christian life, and we situated the field of ethics specifically within the doctrine of salvation. In theological studies, we often refer to salvation as the initial experience that defines when an individual comes to faith. However, salvation technically refers to the whole process of events from one's initial election by God to one's ultimate glorification. Thus, the term salvation is a broad and general term that encompasses a variety of events, such as calling, conviction, repentance, justification, and sanctification, to name a few. In other words, all of these concepts discussed under the doctrine of salvation are part of this idea that we are calling the Christian life. In this chapter, we will flesh out a central component of the Christian life as it relates to our study of the heart of the moral agent: sanctification.[3]

Historical Context

In our previous chapter, we discussed what philosophers call a divine command theory – a version of deontological ethics that grounds the Christian's moral duty in the commands of God. In that chapter, we provided evidence that God has spoken. Because God is the ultimate moral authority, we have a duty to obey his revealed will. Interestingly, not all ethicists affirm the validity of a divine command theory of ethics, and the reasons they cite for rejecting it as a normative ethic vary.

Opposing Divine Command Theory

From Presuppositions about God's Existence

Some, for example, may ground their rejection of divine command theory in their denial of the existence of anything "divine": they may be atheistic or agnostic.[4] If one denies God's existence, then one must necessarily reject revelation as an acceptable epistemological foundation. Consequently, these detractors of divine command theory must also reject as binding any normative ethic that centers on God or his revelation.

From Presuppositions about Commands

Others, however, argue against divine command theory because of their prior philosophical suppositions that commands and ethics are incompatible. Consider the sentiments of Australian philosopher, Graeme de Graff: "There is no room in morality for commands, whether they are the father's, the schoolmaster's, or the priest's. There is still no room for them when they are God's commands."[5] De Graff actually objects to the idea of considering moral imperatives as commands.[6]

From Presuppositions about the Central Task of Ethics

Over the last fifty years, an increasing number of writers have expressed their dissatisfaction with divine command theory based on their understanding of the central task of Christian ethics. Much of the literature in Christian ethics, especially from a deontological perspective, focuses on how Christians should respond to various dilemmas, such as: Is it always wrong to have an abortion? Are Christians permitted to participate in war? Is divorce and remarriage morally permissible? In an attempt to answer these questions, proponents of divine command theory appeal to universal moral norms, such as the moral standards of God.

Opponents of divine command theory argue that "quandary" ethics have wrongly reduced morality to a set of rules and incorrectly construed that ethics primarily addresses actions.[7] In contrast to this focus on doing, this group of opponents to divine command theory posit that the central concern of ethics is: What kind of person should I be? Proponents of this branch of ethics focus on virtue and character formation of the individual rather than a specific conduct of the person faced with a difficult situation.[8]

Philosophically, virtue ethicists draw from the writings of various Greek, Latin, and Christian writings. Chief among these sources are the works of Aristotle and Plato. In their writings, Plato and Aristotle grappled with the idea of a perfect or ideal society. For such a society to exist, it must be composed of citizens who possess an ideal character. In his *Republic*, Plato lists four cardinal virtues that he believes any good citizen of the republic should possess: temperance, fortitude, prudence, and justice. In his *Nichomachean Ethics*, Aristotle expands Plato's list of character traits to eleven, adding virtues like pride, honor, and truthfulness. For Aristotle, these are the virtues that are necessary for individuals to be good citizens of the *polis*.[9] Later writers, such as Cicero, Ambrose, and Augustine included faith, hope, and love, which are often referred to as the theological virtues.[10] Augustine expanded the discussion of virtues by describing the four cardinal virtues as forms of love, namely, love of God.

> Temperance, he reasoned, is love keeping itself entirely and incorrupt for God; fortitude is love bearing everything readily for the sake of God; justice is love serving God only, and therefore, ruling well all else, as subject to man; prudence is love making a right distinction between what helps it towards God and what might hinder it.[11]

In the thirteenth century, Thomas Aquinas systematized much of the earlier discussion. Consequently, he became the primary source for much of the later philosophical and theological discussion on virtues and character.[12]

Most contemporary proponents of virtue ethics find the genesis of their system in the work of Scottish-born philosopher, Alasdair MacIntyre. In his most celebrated work, *After Virtue*, MacIntyre disagreed with what he saw as an erroneous understanding of the nature of ethics: namely, a focus on moral judgments.[13] He attributed this error to a rejection of Aristotle's ethics. In an attempt to correct this error, consequently, he reintroduced this "lost morality of the past", tracing the study of virtue from the time of Homer to the Medieval period.[14] MacIntyre envisioned an ethic that developed within a community and that nurtured a "narrative."[15] This narrative structure, argues MacIntyre, embeds individuals with virtues and enables them to live and pursue the good life. MacIntyre's use of the term narrative is similar to our use of worldview. That is, every ethic is part of a broader interpretive framework that gives meaning and expression to the ethical proposal.

Perhaps the most dominant voice among virtue ethicists in the past fifty years is Stanley Hauerwas, a professor of ethics who spent the majority of his career at Duke University.[16] Like MacIntyre, Hauerwas shares a fundamental commitment to both virtue ethics and the "narrative community."[17] Hauerwas posits that all of human behavior is shaped by the stories of communities. For Hauerwas, the church is the community which tells the story of Jesus Christ, a story that inevitably shapes the thinking, character, and lives of the community's citizens.[18] For Hauerwas, therefore, the task of ethics is to assist the church in being the church[19]— the people in whom "the narrative of God is lived in a way that makes the kingdom visible."[20]

> **Exercise 3.2**: If you enjoy sports, think about the team for which you find yourself cheering. How did you come to choose that team? Were you in any way swayed by the "narrative" in which you were reared? (If you are not into sports, choose another area, such as music, literature, etc.). ∎

Complementing Divine Command Theory

Since MacIntyre's *After Virtue*, the role of character formation and motivation for ethical conduct in the individual have been forefront. For many, virtue ethics firmly reflects the central task of ethics. But this task, as proponents argue, does not support divine command theory; rather, it completely replaces it. This position has two major shortcomings: the rejection of a metanarrative and the rejection of the importance of right conduct in Christian ethics.

First, the "community" narrative that most virtue ethicists advocate denies the existence of a metanarrative – a transcendent narrative that ought to form everyone.[21] In this sense, many virtue ethicists reject any attempt to privilege the Christian narrative in a way that requires all other communities to live out its message. Consequently, this form of virtue ethics reduces to relativism – it is just one story among many.[22] As a result, much of the virtue ethical theory undercuts the absoluteness of the divine command theory.

Secondly, most virtue ethicists reject the supposition that right conduct has an important place in Christian ethics. However, this rejection goes against the history of the church on this position. To be sure, our point about the three parts of morality in chapter one was to show that all three parts have historically been integral to any proper evaluation of the moral agent.

In contrast to those who completely oppose divine command theory, therefore, others view the contributions of virtue ethics as a complement to it. To use John Frame's words, it is another "perspective."[23] Christian ethicist Scott Rae rightly notes, "[V]irtues without principles are blind, but principles without virtues are impotent to motivate people to action."[24] [25]

We have sought to express the discussion of the "heart" of ethics, by which we mean the character of the moral agent, as a necessary part of the moral evaluative process. As such, it complements the duty discussed in the previous chapter.[26] To be sure, we have a duty to be a certain kind of person – one formed in the image of Jesus Christ. To use Hauerwas' terms, we are guided by a Christian narrative or worldview that arises from the Biblical narrative.[27]

What we have highlighted in this historical survey is that living the Christian life well involves more than choosing the right conduct in the midst of a moral dilemma; it also involves the attitude or disposition of the heart. When we speak of the heart of the moral agent, we are referring to a particular kind of person, namely, the kind of person who demonstrates in his decisions and attitude the story of Jesus Christ. Our presentation will follow the path of various virtue ethicists who expand the discussion into three questions: Who are we? Who ought we to become? And, how are we to get there?[28]

> **Exercise 3.3**: Name two competing theories regarding the central task of Christian ethics and discuss the historical and philosophical foundations for how they developed. ■

Begins with Who We Are

In our introduction to the chapter, we located our discussion of the heart of the moral agent within the theological doctrine of sanctification. We do not study business ethics merely in order to discover a proper response to moral dilemmas in the business domain. In business ethics, rather, we examine the Christian life in order to improve the heart, the place where the sanctifying power of God ought to be felt. We study the Christian life to deepen our practice of the Christian life.[29]

The English word sanctification derives from the Latin word *sanctus* which means holy. Consequently, when we discuss sanctification, we could also refer to it as "holi-fication," to coin a new term. Or, to be sanctified, we could call it "holi-fied." To be clear, a discussion on sanctification and the Christian life center around the biblical words holiness, sanctify, and consecrate, all of which derive from the same root word.

Most evangelical treatments in theology sharply distinguish the terms justification and sanctification. In general terms, justification is a legal term that refers to a moment in time when the Moral Ruler of the universe declared one as innocent or in right standing before God on the basis of the gracious gift of the righteousness of Christ being imputed. Sanctification, on the other hand, is often emphasized as a process which occurs in one's life over time.[30] In his book, *Possessed by God*, however, New Testament scholar David Peterson highlights that an important aspect of the biblical usage of sanctification is not a process, but rather, refers to something significant that occurred at the moment of conversion.[31]

Set Apart for God's Purposes

Consider, for example, some of the ways that the term for holy (*qadosh*) is used in the Old Testament. The reader finds the term holy applied to God, to objects in worship, as well as to the people of God. The prophet Isaiah, for example, uses the term holy to denote God's separateness – God is transcendent. "I saw the Lord sitting on his throne, high and lifted up . . . . And one called to another and said, 'Holy, holy, holy is the Lord of Hosts; the whole earth is full of his glory'" (Isa. 6:1,3). Holy, in this sense, refers to God's otherness; he is distinct and separate from the rest of creation.

In the same way, Old Testament writers use the term holy to refer to various objects used in worship. The garments worn by the priests when serving God are holy (Ex. 28:2,4). The tabernacle is called "the holy place," and its innermost portion is called the holy of holies, or "the Most Holy Place" (Ex. 26:33). Even the items offered to God as sacrifices are sacred–set apart for the priests (Lev.22:10). The objects are "holy," "sacred," or "consecrated" because they are "set apart" for God's purposes. The utensils in the temple are not used for eating; they are holy. Thus, the Sabbath day was holy, because it too was set apart for God's purposes.

Not just God and objects used in worship, but even certain individuals affiliated with the Tabernacle were referred to as set apart. When writing about the people of God who were delivered from Egyptian bondage, Moses recorded the words of the Lord: "You shall be to me a kingdom of priests and a holy nation" (Ex. 19:6; Deut. 7:6). This Old Testament use connotes that Israel was different than all the other nations; they were set apart for God's purposes. Therefore, an important aspect of the term sanctification involves the idea of separation.

Set Apart at the Moment of Conversion

We see a similar use of the term in the New Testament. At the moment of conversion, believers are set apart from worldly pursuits. Hence, Paul refers to Christians as "saints" or "holy ones" (Rom. 1:7; I Cor. 1:2). Writing to the church at Corinth, Paul speaks of the incredible transformation that takes place in the person's life. Previously, he said that they were sexually immoral, idolaters, adulterers, greedy, and drunkards. But now, he refers to them as "washed" and "sanctified" (I Cor. 6:11). These believers have a new status and identity because of the work of Jesus Christ. The writer of Hebrews is equally clear: "We have been sanctified through the offering of the body of Jesus Christ once for all" (Heb. 10:10).

Summary

Thus, we can summarize an important aspect of sanctification as positional. It is something that describes who we are in Christ: we are sanctified. In this sense, we have been set apart for God's purposes. But this is not the only way in which the term is used in Scripture. Indeed,

God's willingness to set us apart – to sanctify us – carries with it a demand to live up to this new status (Lev. 11:45). We now turn to the second use of the term.

Pursues Who We Ought to Become

Not only do biblical authors use the term holy to connote being separate, they also employ the term in a manner that signifies moral purity. Indeed, this moral purity appears to be part of the purpose for which we were set apart.

Pursues Moral Purity

The pursuit of moral purity among those whom God has set apart is linked to the character of God and one's desire to maintain fellowship with God. Consider, for instance, the prophet Habakkuk's description of God. "Are you not from everlasting, O Lord my God, my Holy One? . . . You who are of purer eyes than to see evil and cannot look at wrong" (Hab.1:12-13). Because of the degree to which God is holy, he cannot abide in the presence of sin. The writer of Leviticus underscores this truth, as well as the obligation that follows being separated: "For I am the Lord who brought you up out of the land of Egypt to be your God. You shall therefore be holy, for I am holy" (Lev. 11:45).

Not only is the Christian's pursuit of holiness linked with God's holy character, it is also linked to one's desire to maintain fellowship with God. The Psalmist asks: "Who shall ascend the hill of the Lord? And who shall stand in his holy place? He who has clean hands and a pure heart, who does not lift up his soul to what is false and does not swear deceitfully" (Ps. 24:3-4). Thus, Scripture links fellowship with a holy God to the individual's duty to live a morally holy life. We see these two aspects of holiness in the history of God's people in the Old Testament. When they did not live apart from other nations as God had commanded them, then they began to adopt the practices of the people with whom they lived; they began to worship their gods and fall deeply into moral degradation.

New Testament writers show that Christians were called to live out their new status in a way that was distinctively different. In addition, the New Testament authors identify the means for how this holiness is accomplished. Paul, for example, suggests that the work of the Holy Spirit is the primary way in which believers are made holy. In his letter to the church at Rome, Paul connected the work of the Holy Spirit with the acceptability of the Gentiles' offerings to God (Rom. 15:16). In a similar fashion, Paul associates the sanctification of the people in Thessalonica with the work of the Spirit: "But we ought always to give thanks to God for you, brothers beloved by the Lord, because God chose you as the first fruits to be saved, through sanctification by the Spirit and belief in the truth" (II Thes. 2:13).

Within our discussion of the heart of the moral agent, therefore, we see two extremely important concepts for ethics that flow from the doctrine of sanctification. First, who we are as Christians begins with the work of God: he sets us apart. Secondly, he sets us apart for a reason: to live differently from the rest of the world. While there is a sense of personal responsibility in living the morally pure life (Phil. 2:12-13; Heb. 12:14; Col. 3:12-13), it is ultimately the work of the Holy Spirit that produces his fruits in our lives (Gal. 5:22-23). The Spirit empowers individuals to pursue holiness and to live rightly.

Pursues Christlike Character

The New Testament further refines what moral purity looks like: Christlikeness. Indeed, the New Testament writers imply that Christlikeness was God's intention from the moment of predestination (Rom. 8:29) to the moment of glorification (1 John 3:2). Christlikeness–being conformed to the image of Jesus Christ–is primarily being like Christ in our hearts: having a Christlike character.

Character of Christian Leaders

We have a beautiful picture of Christlike character in the New Testament in passages that deal with Christian leaders. What these passages show us is that the chief qualification for Christian leadership is character. From our perspective, we might say it this way: the central qualification for doing business ethically–being a Christian business person–is character. In two foundational passages on leadership, Paul makes clear that character is more important than gifts, experience, or education. That is, leaders are not simply called to live according to a higher standard. To be sure, we are all called to be like Christ. Christian leaders are supposed to represent those who have made significant progress toward this goal of being like Christ that they can serve as examples to others (I Pet. 5:3). In the two central passages about leaders (1 Tim. 3:1-7; Titus 1:5-9), Paul provides a list of character traits expected of Christian leaders. But these lists were in no way meant to be exhaustive, but rather, indicative of the areas in which we might exhibit Christlikeness. Writing to different audiences, we are not surprised the Paul repeats several traits. We can summarize these traits into the following five groups.

• **Commitment to Moral Excellence:** In both passages, Paul writes that "overseer" or the "elder . . . must be above reproach" (1 Tim. 3:2; Titus 1:6). In the context of Paul's letters to Timothy and Titus, he was addressing pastors. In our immediate discussion, however, we are expanding this discussion to persons of leadership more broadly. Commitment to moral excellence implies that the individual does not see how close to temptation he may walk without committing sin. To the contrary, those committed to excellence strive to avoid morally questionable behavior at all costs. The thought of "average Christianity" has absolutely zero appeal. Rather, being a person that is "above reproach" suggests a commitment to moral excellence—going beyond the minimum requirements. Paul uses a number of words to paint the picture of one committed to moral excellence. In fact, the rest of the list details this pursuit of moral excellence.

• **Commitment to Faithfully Fulfill Family Responsibilities:** A second important character trait for followers of Christ is a commitment to fulfill family responsibilities. Two areas where this might be lived out and applied are with regard to one's spouse and with regard to one's children. When Paul speaks of "the husband of one wife," for example, he is not concerned so much with avoiding polygamy or assigning unmarried individuals to a second class of leadership (1 Tim. 3:2). Rather, the question is this: Can this individual serve as an example of one who faithfully fulfills his responsibilities as a Christian husband? Certainly the whole of Scripture stands against the idea of polygamy, and so Paul too would not have supported it. But I am far pressed to conclude that such an issue is what most attracted his attention at this point. Similarly, Paul addressed favorably in both Corinthians and Romans the idea of a widow being permitted to marry again. But whether it is a widow, a single person, or a married individual, Paul's primary contention is whether or not the person is "above reproach" in the area of marriage fidelity. Concerning the widow, for example, when one inspects the whole of his life and how he lived with his spouse while she lived, did he faithfully fulfill his God-ordained responsibilities to her? Christlike character cannot be divorced — to use a pun — from one's responsibilities to his or her spouse.

Christlike character not only is displayed in how we relate to our spouse, but also in how we "manage" our children (1 Tim. 3:4; Titus 1:6). Do our children reflect that they have been taught Christlike character, such as a submissive spirit? Do we manage our household in a manner that is characterized by dignity (or reverence, seriousness, holiness, probity)? Scripture is absolutely devoid of any idea that children should do as they please. What is clear from the two lists is that the family is an important arena for where Christlike character is both developed and revealed.

• **Commitment to Self-Control:** Thirdly, Christlike character reflects self-control. In Paul's letters to Timothy and Titus, he states that the character of Christ evidenced in the maturing believer will not be "violent" "quarrelsome," (1 Tim. 3:3), nor "quick-tempered." (Tit. 1:7). Rather, the response of one whose character has been shaped by the indwelling Spirit will demonstrate "gentleness" or "forbearance" (1 Tim. 3:3). Thus, one has reached the level of maturity that he is not controlled by his appetites. Hence, the individual is not given to drunkenness. Because the list is not exhaustive, I believe that we can safely add that the self-control would exclude gluttony, laziness, lust, or any other negative appetite.

• **Commitment to Service:** Fourthly, the one who is growing in Christlike character will evidence such progress in service to others. Paul uses the term "hospitable" (1 Tim. 3:2; Tit.1:8). The emphasis seems to be that the Christlike person is concerned with others and is not always self-focused. In management, we often speak of servant leadership, which demonstrates itself in service to others.

• **Commitment to Integrity:** Finally, Christlike character demands integrity. By this term, I am attempting to capture Paul's spirit that the Christian leader make the right decision even when it is not comfortable and easy to do so. Hence, Paul exhorts Timothy and Titus to be "above reproach," "respectful," "trustworthy," "upright," "holy," and "disciplined" (Tit.1). Collectively, Paul calls leaders to be people of integrity.

Character of the Holy Spirit

Another passage that I believe accurately and faithfully summarizes the character traits of those who are following Christ is in Paul's letter to the Galatians. In the passage on the "fruits of the Spirit," Paul list nine important traits that reflect the Spirit's working in an individual's life: "love, joy, peace, patience, kindness, goodness, faithfulness, gentleness, [and] self-control" (Gal. 5:22-23). Many of these traits resemble the character of godly leaders. That is, one does not have to strain very hard to see that gentleness in the fruits of the spirit is linked with self-control in 1 Timothy. Similarly, faithfulness is linked with integrity and family responsibilities. Clearly, one whose life is characterized by the fruits of the spirit could be said to be "above reproach."

Character of Love

A final passage on Christlike character is 1 Corinthians 13 in which Paul discusses the nature of love. In this passage, Paul seeks to describe love in three different ways: what it is, what is not, and what it does.

First, he provides two positive statements about what love is: "love is patient and kind" (1 Cor. 13:4). Secondly, Paul uses eight negatives to describe what love does not do: "love does not envy or boast; it is not arrogant or rude. It does not insist on its own way; it is not irritable or resentful; it does not rejoice at wrongdoing" (1 Cor. 13:4-6).

Finally, Paul notes five positives that love does: "rejoices with the truth. Love bears all things, believes all things, hopes all things, and endures all things" (1 Cor. 13:6-7). In each of these descriptions, Paul emphasizes the verbal nature of love over the idea of it being a fuzzy feeling. Paul uses action terms: love rejoices, bears, believes, and endures.

In other passages of Scripture, we see that love is the linchpin between right conduct and right heart. This love which acts as Paul describes in 1 Corinthians flows from a particular type of character. That is, Paul describes a certain kind of person who is characterized by a particular conduct: the person rejoices, bears, endures, and hopes. More importantly, Paul argues that this kind of behavior flows from a particular kind of person: one who is patient and kind, not given to envy or boasting, etc. Who we are – our character – affects what we do – our behavior. Similarly, how we conduct ourselves informs others about our character. In 1 Corinthians, Paul uses the term love to describe both the character and the conduct. In his passage on the fruits of the Spirit, Paul similarly uses love as a summary of the other nine traits, similar to Augustine's use of love as a summary virtue.[32] In contrast to the contemporary use of love a fuzzy feeling, therefore, Scripture presents love as a choice: a choice regarding the character of our being and the nature of our actions.

> **Exercise 3.4**: List some of the character traits that Scripture uses to describe the heart or character of one who is being formed into the image of Jesus Christ. Does the existence of these character traits guarantee that one will have right conduct? If not, what is the relationship between these character traits and right ethical conduct? ∎

Chooses to Love

Having been set apart by God for a particular purpose – to be Christlike – Christians are enabled through the power of the Holy Spirit to accept God's election on their lives; they can choose to love. Jesus' discourse with a religious lawyer helps us to understand better this connection between love as a character trait and love as a duty which we can choose to accept or reject. Matthew records:

> But when the Pharisees heard that he had silenced the Sadducees, they gathered together. And one of them, a lawyer, asked him a question to test him. "Teacher, which is the great commandment in the Law?" And he said to him, "You shall love

the Lord your God with all your heart and with all your soul and with all your mind. This is the great and first commandment. And a second is like it: You shall love your neighbor as yourself. On these two commandments depend all the Law and the Prophets. (Matt. 22:34-40)

In his replay to the expert in the law, therefore, Jesus summarized the whole duty of man with one word: love. Moreover, Jesus states that this love should be directed toward God (Deut. 6:5) and toward others (Lev. 19:18).

If we turn to Deuteronomy from which Jesus is quoting, we make an interesting discovery. In context, God's call to love is introduced as: "Now this is the commandment – the statues and the rules – that the Lord your God commanded you" (Deut. 6:1). Next, Moses supplements God's command with words like "do them" (6:1), "keep" them (6:2), and "obey" them (6:3). Thus, the Bible clearly expresses love as a duty.

Loves God

Recall that in chapter two, we stated that right conduct springs from our duty to God's revelation. Moreover, this duty to obey may be fulfilled in our "keeping" and "doing" the law – in our behavior – as well as in our imitating God – in our being or character. This command to love God is not burdensome. Rather, the whole biblical narrative paints a picture of God's action on behalf of his people that propels us to obey: to love. If Hauerwas is correct and we are formed by the stories of our community – the church – then we cannot help but become a people characterized by love. Our story, which is found in the Holy Scriptures, proclaims a God who is fundamentally good. He provides food, water, and shelter (Ps. 104:10-28), even down to the most insignificant of creatures: birds and grass (Mt. 6:26-30). But for those created in his image, God's display of love is even greater. God called Abraham and entered into a covenant with him to redeem the same people who disobeyed and rejected him. The apostle Paul summarizes God's actions on our behalf this way: "For you know the grace of our Lord Jesus Christ, that though he was rich, yet for your sake he became poor, so that you by his poverty, might become rich" (2 Cor. 8:9). In another passage, Paul stated, "but God showed his love for us in that while we were still sinners, Christ died for us" (Rom. 5:8). Thus, while it is a command, it is not onerous. We joyfully love the one "who first loved us" (1 John. 4:19).

But love is also an attribute of God: "God is love" (1 John. 4:8). Therefore, we glorify and please the Father when we imitate God. But we also imitate God when we love others. Indeed, our love for God propels us to love others. John writes, "We have this command from Him: The one who loves God must also love his brother" (1 John 4:21). Love of God leads to love of neighbor.

Loves Neighbor

Just as our love for God could be fulfilled in our doing and in our being, so also can the duty to love our neighbor. Jesus calls the love of neighbor the second great commandment: "You shall love your neighbor as yourself" (Matt, 22:39). In stating this command, Jesus is merely quoting the Old Testament law (Lev. 19:18), which falls in the midst of the Holiness Code (Lev. 17 - 26). God is holy and God is love, and we imitate him when we have lives characterized by holiness and exemplified in love for God and love for others.

In fact, love for God and love for neighbor are not just another command or law. Rather, Jesus states that love for God and love for others summarizes the whole Old Testament law (Matt. 22:40). We see in this truth reflected in two ways. First, many writers have noted how the Ten Commandments – the heart of God's law – may be divided into two groups: those which more directly address how we relate to God (commandments 1 - 4) and those that more clearly address how we relate to others (commandments 5 - 10). Thus, the commands that confront us with absolute loyalty to God alone and keeping the Sabbath clearly relate to our relationship with God. Equally clear, commandments about avoiding adultery, lying, and murder concern primarily our relationship with others. Thus, the Ten Commandments seem to illustrate that the moral standards of God can be summarized in love for God and love for neighbor.[33]

In his letter to the church at Rome, Paul confirms this reading. He writes:

Owe no one anything, except to love each other, for the one who loves another has fulfilled the law. For the commandments, "You shall not commit adultery, You shall not murder, You shall not steal, You shall not covet," and any other commandment, are summed up in this word: You shall love your neighbor as yourself. Love does no wrong to neighbor; therefore love is the fulfilling of the law." (Rom. 13:8-10)

Summary

Love, therefore, truly is the linchpin between right heart and right conduct. It not only summarizes our moral duty to love God and to love neighbor, but it also summarizes the motivation and character of one who seeks to fulfill these moral standards. In his *Introduction to Biblical Ethics*, Christian ethicist David W. Jones assists us in evaluating the heart of the moral agent with the question: "Am I acting out of love for God and love for neighbor?"[34] Such introspection, Jones rightly notes, is the hallmark of Christian character.

Is Nurtured through Cooperation

At the beginning of this chapter, we noted that various virtue ethicists divide their discussion of ethics into three questions: Who are we? What kind of person ought I to become? And finally, How do we get there? Up to this point, we have answered the first two questions. Who we are begins with God separating us for his purposes. God's desire is that through the sanctification process, we become Christlike. So the final question involves this: How is Christlike character developed?

God Initiates

In the second part of John Bunyan's famous, *Pilgrim's Progress*, the author tells the story of three travelers: Mercy, Matthew, and Christiana. The three are attempting to cross the Delectable Mountains after escaping the Giants of Despair. Upon entering the Shepherd's Palace, Mercy discovers a Mirror. As Bunyan develops the story, this mirror is truly wonderful. When one gazes into the mirror from the front, it seems like any other mirror. One sees the reflection of self with the normal blemishes. When one looks at the mirror from the back, however, something miraculous occurs. Rather than reflecting self, the mirror "shows one the very Face and Similitude of the Prince of Pilgrims himself."[35] Anyone who seeks to see the person in the mirror from the reverse side, therefore, only sees the image of Jesus Christ.

Like the wonderful mirror, our progress in holiness is not so much what we can achieve, but who we can reflect. That is, our progress reflects the grace of God.[36] Like salvation, Christian character begins with God: namely, his grace. Paul provides us various ways in which God, through grace, plays a significant role in our growth.[37] Writing to Titus, Paul noted that grace "trains" us (negatively) to renounce ungodliness and (positively) to pursue holiness (Titus 2:11-14). Paul reminds the Christians in Corinth that God's Spirit transforms them. And in the famous Christ hymn in Philippians, Paul tells us that it is God, through his grace, that works in us to enable us to even desire godliness (Phil. 2:13). Truly, real growth in Christlike character begins with the work of God.

By God's initiative, we are placed on the road to holiness. To use the biblical metaphor, we were dead before he acted. Nevertheless, he provides the seed, plants the seed, and ultimately produces the fruit. Hence, this new character in us is the fruit of "the Spirit." Ultimately, Paul writes, it is God "who makes things grow" (1 Cor. 3:7).

Individuals Cooperate

God also enlists human cooperation in the sanctification process. He does not do this because he needs our assistance, but rather, because he honors us as responsible moral agents. This truth is made clear in the subtitle to Jerry Bridges book on holiness: "God's Role and Our Role in the Pursuit of Holiness."[38] Several passages in the Pauline corpus reinforce this conclusion that real growth in godliness requires both divine and human action (1 Cor. 15:10; Gal.2:19-21; Phil. 2:12-13; Rom. 15:15-19; 2 Cor. 9:8-9).[39] Human cooperation may involve various stages.

• **Accept:** To return to the metaphor of a garden, if God is the one who plants, then our first step is reception; we must accept what God has planted in us. As James writes, "Put away all filthiness and rampant wickedness and receive with meekness the implanted word" (James 1:21).

• **Submission:** Secondly, growth in Christlikeness involves our submission. John states that the grain of what that falls must "die" in order to reproduce. In this context, our "dying" is to self and submitting to the filling of the Holy Spirit.

• **Cultivation:** The final two ways in which humans cooperate are integrally related. In keeping with the gardening metaphor, we can use the term cultivation to refer to the removal of weeds: those things in our life that might choke out the Spirit's work (Mk. 4:18-19). The Puritans referred to this process of removing weeds mortification: killing sin. In his book, *Mortification of Sin*, puritan author John Owen begins with an explication of Romans 8.[40] In that passage, Paul writes: "For if you live according to the flesh you will die, but if by the Spirit you put to death the deeds of the body, you will live" (Rom. 8:13). The idea of mortification comes from Paul's statement about "putting to death."[41]

• **Fertilization:** The idea of cultivation, or putting to death, connotes ridding ourselves of those things that hinder our growth. In addition to removing sinful influences, however, we need to "put on" certain things. Various means exist through which we can stimulate growth in our walk with Christ. Some of these disciplines include prayer, Bible study, fellowship, and service.[42] It is important to see that these activities–prayer, Bible study, evangelism, etc.–are not merely activities in which people with good character participate, although this may be true. Rather, these are the activities that help to inculcate a good, Christlike character: they are the means of grace.

Summary

In this chapter, we have argued that ethics is more than behavior. One can "do" the right thing and still not have acted ethically if the action itself sprang from a corrupt heart. We highlighted a particular stream of ethical theory that asserts that the central task of ethics is with the character and virtue of the moral agent. And, while we disagreed with particular suppositions of this theory, such as its rejection of any focus on conduct and its rejection of the priority of the Christian narrative, we nevertheless acknowledged Scripture's teaching on the importance of character.

Consequently, we outlined how this right character begins with God's decision to separate us for his purposes and how it is cultivated through various disciplines. Moreover, we emphasized the inherent link between who we are (i.e., our character) and how we live (i.e., our actions).

Chapter 4:
Right Purpose in Business Ethics

After graduating from college, Henry Kaestner worked for industry-leading firms like Arthur Anderson and Merrill Lynch. Despite having considerable success at these jobs, evidenced by higher salaries and bigger houses, Kaestner admits that he was not happy. His continued trek to success led him to Chapel Hill, North Carolina where he sought to establish his own brokerage firm.

While living in North Carolina, Kaestern began attending a local Presbyterian Church. Through the ministries of this church, Kaestner's perspectives on life and business began to change. Not too long after his move to North Carolina, Kaestner and his friend David Morken started a new company called Bandwidth.com. The idea was to establish a company with an environment where a person of conviction could flourish in the marketplace without feeling that his convictions were compromised. Kaestner said that he wanted to demonstrate that faith and principles were not incompatible with running a successful business.

After two years of not posting any revenue, a sales person landed the company its first major contract. However, the company soon learned that the client was involved in online pornography and online scamming. At that moment, Kaestner and Morken had to make a decision about the principles of their company. They made a decision that made little sense financially at that time. Kaestner killed the deal, but he still paid full commission to the salesperson who brought the client, since the salesperson had followed completely all company protocols. Over the next four years (2003 - 2007), Bandwidth.com was the fourth fastest growing privately owned company in America. A spinoff company, Republic Wireless was launched and handled all of Google's voice operations.

The founding values of Bandwidth.com were: faith, family, work, and fitness. By the time Kaestner left the company, he was pleased to see that he had successfully been faithful to these values. With regard to family, the company had a generous paid leave program. With regard to fitness, nearly two-thirds of its nearly 500 employees worked out every day at lunch. The company supported dozens of service projects and Bible studies at its Durham campus and raised funds for organizations like Big Brothers and Big Sisters, Meals on Wheels, as well as funds for landscaping local parks.

> **Exercise 4.1**: From the introductory story, name a moral agent. What clues from the story demonstrate the moral agent's love for God and love for community? ∎

In our introduction, we mentioned that in our ethical evaluation of a moral event, there must be three parts. In previous chapters, we discussed the importance of right conduct and a right heart. In this chapter, we want to examine the third component of morality: namely, a right purpose. In our discussion of right conduct, we used the technical term "deontological" to describe an approach to ethics that focuses on one's duty. In broad terms, we use the term "teleological" to refer to an approach to ethics that focuses on the goal or purpose. The term 'teleological' comes from the Greek *telos*, meaning end, goal, or purpose. Thus, teleological ethics concerns itself with goals, purposes, or ends.

In Historical Context

If we were to do a brief survey of secular philosophy, we would see two pronounced interpretations of ethics: naturalism and idealism. Whereas idealism emphasizes the priority of the mind and the reality of a spiritual world, naturalism in contrast tends to stress the non-supernatural and treats humans as nothing more than a rational animal. Nearly all of secular ethics can be classified into one of these two major systems. Regardless of the categorization, ironically, philosophers in each system struggled to identify an adequate principle for life conduct.

Naturalistic Theories of Ethics

Epicureanism

In this section, it is not my intention to do a survey of ancient philosophy. Rather, I intend to show a common theme among the different philosophies. Consider for example, the rule of life proposed by Epicurus (341 - 270 B.C.). Epicureanism modified the Cyrenaic morality, which insisted that the guiding principle for one's life was the execution of whatever yields maximum pleasure: "eat, drink, and be merry." In its place, Epicurus advocated pursuing long-term, mental pleasures. Epicurus explained the "good life" in terms of pleasure versus pain, advocating those activities that produced more fruitful and long-range pleasures. Because not all pleasures are equal, Epicurus introduced a new idea into the definition: the absence of pain. If the pursuit of pleasure is the highest good, Epicurus reasoned that pain must be the greatest evil. Thus, Epicureanism teaches, a wise hedonist will choose that which gives the greatest pleasure and the least pain. Consequently, Epicurus believed that pleasures of the mind were superior to pleasures of the body, because bodily pleasures involved some pain (thirst, hunger, full). Moreover, pleasures of the mind tended to last longer.

Because Epicureanism advocates repressing short-term, immediate, pleasures of the flesh for long-term, mental pleasures, followers are possibly faced with a dilemma; they may die and thus experience neither. As a result, Epicureanism leads to pessimism. In conclusion, Epicureanism, by subscribing to a naturalistic worldview, not only results in a non-Christian picture of humanity (qualitatively equal to the beast), but also requires relativistic ethic—an obvious product of removing God, the supreme Moral Ruler, from one's view of reality.

From a moral perspective, the problem is clear. One does not choose long-term pleasures because God approves them or because they lead to future rewards, such as heaven, but rather, because they turn nature to one's advantage (egoistic). Likewise, one does not repress short-term pleasures, such as lust, because God (the moral Ruler) condemns such actions, but rather because they frustrate one's ability to live the Epicurean philosophy. Notice that for Epicureanism, as for most naturalistic worldviews, there are no oughts, only what is.

Utilitariansim

In chapter two, we mentioned an approach to ethics called Utilitarianism. Utilitarianism is a modern version of Epicureanism. One of the original champions of Utilitarianism said of Epicurus: "He is the only one among the ancients who had the merit of having known the true source of morality."[1] The two leading proponents for utilitarianism were Jeremy Bentham and John Stuart Mill. Both men maintained naturalistic worldviews similar to Epicurus. From their worldview, humans are viewed as a rational animal, not dissimilar to views of Epicurus. As such, they proposed analyzing ethical situations by scientific calculation. Their aim was to make morals as accurate as physics. Through the exercise of various criteria for measuring the rightness or wrongness of a possible act, such as intensity, duration, certainty, purity, and number of persons affected, Utilitarianism's approach to distinguishing right from wrong becomes "as rational as mathematics.

Not only is Utilitarianism overly rationalistic, it also is highly altruistic. Unlike Epicureanism, Utilitarianism does not seek short or long-term pleasures for the individual (egoism), but rather the "greatest happiness of the greatest number of people." For Utilitarianism, the ends (results) justify the means. To discredit this worldview, therefore, one need only show how some pleasurable consequences can lead to embarrassing results. Consider the following story by Nash:

> Imagine two worlds: In world one, the leaders arrest a small group of individuals, torture them, and kill them. For reasons unknown, the majority of people receive great pleasure from this act. In world two, the citizens are all treated justly, but the majority of the people sense less pleasure than those in world one. According to Utilitarianism, world one is the more just society.[2]

In both systems, Epicureanism and Utilitarianism, the "good life" is stated in terms of some reward: happiness. For Epicureanism, it was a self-centered happiness – that which gives "me" the greatest pleasure. In Utilitarianism, it was more altruistic–that which brings the greatest happiness to the greatest number of people. Either way, external rewards, such as happiness, motivate the moral agent.

Idealistic Theories of Ethics

Plato

The movement from Naturalism to Idealism did not result in a complete rejection of naturalistic premises. Rather, Idealists appear to accept as true various aspects of Naturalism, but they add a caveat. Metaphysically, for example, Idealists do not reject the physical world; they simply assert that is not the only reality or possibly the ultimate reality. With regard to anthropology, Idealists do not deny that humans are an animal, but rather, this physical reality does not exhaust humanity's personality. Most importantly for our discussion, the two major philosophical systems also part ways with regard to ethics. Because naturalist ethics reject any idea of a transcendent being, morality becomes subjective and relative. Idealists, on the other hand, believe in absolutes and unchanging standards. When one moves from Naturalism to Idealism, one moves from the pursuit of the good life for its mere rewards to seeking it because it is essentially better.

In many regards, Plato is the archetypal Idealist. Born in 427 B.C. in Athens, his parents gave him the name Aristocles. Plato's worldview differed greatly from that of the naturalistic philosophers. Metaphysically, he did not deny the existence of the materialistic world. Rather, Plato argued that true reality included an immaterial world of ideas. For Plato, in fact, the sphere of ideas or "forms" was more real than the physical world.

In book 7 of his *Republic*, Plato writes about a group of prisoners who live in a cave. The way he describes the story, the prisoners are situated at the back of the cave and chained in such a manner that they cannot see anything behind them. At some distance behind the prisoners lies a wall and a fire. Between the wall and the fire people can walk and carry small statues, which result in the shadows of the statues appearing on the wall of the cave before the eyes of the prisoners. The prisoners know nothing of the wall, the people, the statues, or the fire. To them, the shadows are the real world.

Plato entertains the possibility of one of the prisoners escaping and learning about the world that exists outside of the cave. When the freed individual returns to tell the prisoners about the other world, the prisoners refuse to believe him and resent being told that their understanding of the world is not real. Ultimately, the prisoners kill the individual.

In the story, the prisoners represent the physical world – the world of naturalistic philosophy. It is the world of particulars. It is the world that the prisoners had experienced. We could describe their epistemology as empiricism. What they understood to be real was based upon their sense experience. In the story, Plato invites the people to imagine a world that is not experienced yet is real. The world outside the cave, and even the fire itself, represent this other world – what he calls the world of forms or ideas. Hence, Plato rejected both the metaphysical conclusions of naturalism – that this material world is all that there is – and the epistemological claim that humans can adequately discern truth through empiricism.

These two worldview claims consequently affected his understanding of the "good life." Plato rejected hedonistic claims that pleasure is the greatest good. To be sure, his understanding of the good life flowed from his beliefs about the world of forms. When most people think about Plato and forms, they describe his philosophy in terms of some ideal horse or dog. For example, one might imagine that in the world of forms there exists an ideal dog. And on this world of particulars, we see dogs of many sizes and shapes, from Great Danes to Poodles. Nevertheless, when we see a dog we recognize that is in fact a dog and not a horse, perhaps as a result of us having in our minds this idea of the ideal dog. What is important for our discussion on ethics, however, is that while Plato might have imagined an ideal horse, or dog, or even an ideal table, what truly captured his mind was the idea of an ideal form of Truth, Beauty, Justice, and Good.

In his *Euthyphro*, Plato writes that Euthyphro attempts to define these terms. Yet, instead of defining the term, such as justice, he merely offered examples. If Euthyphro were describing the term love for a contemporary audience, he might say it is a warm feeling inside, the feeling a husband has for his wife, buying chocolate for another, and flowers on special occasions. Instead of these examples, however, Euthyphro's teacher Socrates wants to know what these examples have in common. That is, the common thread is the essential meaning of love. For Plato, the example extends to the ideas of Good and Right. We can think of examples of Good and Right, but the meaning and essence of Good is what the examples have in common. And this essence is universal, absolute, and unchanging. Thus, Plato and the Idealists not only the reject the hedonistic ethics of Naturalism, they likewise rebuff their relativism. Right, Good, and Just are absolute and unchanging for Idealists.

One final note about Plato's philosophy springs from his hierarchical view of the universe. We have already noted that he believed in a world of particulars and a world of forms. The particulars, of course, refer to the physical or material world. The world of forms refers to Plato's understanding of the immaterial world – the world of universals. However, Plato further bifurcated the world of forms. Situated at the apex of Plato's universe was the highest of all forms, the Good. In Plato's Republic, Socrates asserts that the Good is the ultimate end of human life.

Aristotle

When one moves from Naturalism to Idealism, one moves from the pursuit of the good life for its mere rewards to seeking it because it is essentially better. Aristotle represents a second example of an idealistic ethic. In his *Nichomachean Ethics*, Aristotle notes that all of human action is directed toward an ultimate end or goal.[3] Aristotle argues that humans intentionally act with the intent of accomplishing a particular objective. Accordingly, Aristotle questions whether or not there exists a particular goal that is superior to all other goals. For Aristotle this single highest goal for every human is *eudaemonia*, which is often translated as "happiness." However, the translation of "happiness" does not fully connote the idealistic aspect of the good life. Consequently, Jones suggests using the term "flourishing," and Frame recommends "blessedness."[4] The idea behind these new translations is that the good life involves more than an emotional state, such as happiness. Rather, it includes benefits to one's life that results in true happiness.

Thus, whether it is Naturalism or Idealism, every philosopher asserts that humans are seeking happiness. French theologian, Blaise Pascal (1623–1662) summarized the pursuit of the good life well when he wrote: "All people are in search of happiness. There is no exception to this whatever different methods are employed."[5] And finally, Jonathan Edwards echoed these sentiments writing, "saints and sinners, and all alike, love happiness, and have the same unalterable and instinctive inclination to desire and seek it."[6]

Augustine

In his treatise, "On the Morals of the Catholic Church," Augustine described four groups of people who seek the life of happiness. Of the four individuals, Augustine argues that three cannot ever be truly happy. Describing the three who will not be happy, he writes:

> But the title happy cannot, in my opinion, belong either to him who has not what he loves, whatever it may be, or to him who has what he loves if it is hurtful, or to him who does not love what he has, although it is good in perfection.[7]

The first person, Augustine asserts, cannot be happy because he does not possess the things that he wants most in life. In other words, this person longs for some thing, some person, or even some achievement, but the thing pursued lies outside of his grasp. As result, the person cannot be happy.

Augustine describes a second kind of person who also will not be happy. Unlike the first person, this second person can actually attain what he loves. However, what he loves is not good for him. In his book on *Reordered Love*, Christian author David Naugle comments on this second kind of person. He summarizes this individual with the words from a country-western song by Alan Jackson:

> Everything I love is killing me, Cigarettes, Jack Daniels and caffeine; And that's the way you're turning out to be; Everything I love, you have to give it up, 'Cause everything I love is killing me.[8]

Augustine simply describes the third type of unhappy person as one who has what should make him happy, but he nevertheless does not find enjoyment in it. The individual does not value that which is actually valuable.

Augustine describes these three kinds of unhappy individuals as tortured, cheated, or diseased because they either cannot obtain what they love, love what they should not, or they simply do not love what they ought to love.[9] One may wonder if happiness is unattainable since these three could not achieve it. Consequently, Augustine describes a fourth individual who indeed is happy. This happiness occurs according to Augustine "when that which is man's chief good is both loved and possessed."[10] Philosophers call this "chief end" to which Augustine refers the *summum bonum*. Again, David Naugle concludes that genuine happiness depends upon one knowing what this *summum bonum* is, having it in one's life, and loving it with all of one's heart. The driving question for the individual becomes, therefore, "What is the chief end? What is the highest good?" In contemporary vernacular, we might ask it this way: What is genuinely in my interest, and how can I truly be well off? What is the good life and who is a truly good person?[11]

> **Exercise 4.2**: In this first section, we outlined two major interpretations for ethics: Naturalism and Idealism. In addition, we reviewed how each interpretation leads to a different understanding of what is "good" and "right" and "just." In the business world, where do you see examples of the naturalistic and idealistic philosophies being lived out? List two examples of individuals who seem to follow naturalistic and two examples of individuals who followed idealistic philosophies in the business world. ∎

Influenced by One's Worldview

Just based on what we have seen so far, one's understanding of the good life and the highest good arise from one's worldview. What we believe about the world's structures and ultimate reality determine our perspective on the meaning and purpose of life. Philosophers like Epicurus, Bentham, and Mill held to a naturalistic worldview in which they denied the existence of God (or God's ability to affect us in the natural world). Moreover, humans were viewed as mere rational animals. With this worldview, it is not surprising that the highest good involves pleasures situated in this world. If one is a Naturalist, then one must receive his reward here and now; there is no other time or place for it. One's view of happiness is inextricably tied to one's worldview. Consider the following chart.[12]

Table 1: Worldivew and Happiness

Worldview	View of Happiness
Theism	Loving God as Creator and Redeemer
Deism	Be good, revere a transcendent God
Pantheism	Living in harmony with the divine cosmos
Polytheism	Placating the gods and goddesses
Naturalism	Exalting self and enjoying the world
Materialism	Pleasures and consumption
Existentialism	Authenticity by choices
Spiritualism	Consciousness expansion, meditation
Paganism	Devotion to gods of self, sex, the occult, environment, etc

In contrast to secular philosophers, Augustine approached the question from a Biblical worldview. For Augustine, God is the One who stands at the top of the hierarchy of reality.[13] Accordingly, Augustine argued, God is our *summum bonum*:[14]

> God is the supreme good, by reference to which all our actions are directed. It is the good we seek for itself and not because of something else, and once it is attained, we seek nothing further to make us happy. This, in fact, is what we call it our end, because other things are desired on account of this *summum bonum*, while it is desired purely for itself.[15]

Influenced by Culture

What we have just argued is that our view of the good life or the chief end of humanity springs from our worldview. Secondly however the culture in which we live also influences our understanding of the good life. In the music we hear, the commercials that we see, and through the commentaries that we consume on the Internet, all have the capacity to shape our understanding of the good life.

In our contemporary culture, where so few grapple with the nature of truth, celebrities often become the authority figures for our understanding of the good life. Naugle rightly notes that celebrities "train us well about things like sex, food, fashion, money, possessions, achievement, prestige, and power."[16] As a result of culture's influence, many have had their moral compasses reprogrammed. They fail to evaluate rightly what is good. After the Apostle Paul met Jesus on the road to Damascus, he too realized that many of the things that he thought were good and important were really "rubbish" (Phil 3:8). Too many people around us have confused rubbish for the good life. The Psalmist echoes this point when he asks, "O men, how long shall my honor be turned into shame? How long will you love vain words and seek after lies?" (Ps. 4:2) In other words, the world proposes a plethora of substitutes for the good life. However, the Bible's assessment of their proposals is that they are lies and rubbish. Author William Cowper aptly writes, "What is base no polish can make sterling."[17]

As a result of our needs and because of the influence of culture, we love many things. And while it certainly is possible that we love some things that we should hate, it is also possible that we love some things that are good. To be sure, God has provided a multiplicity of means for meeting our needs. Because they are created by God and are provided by God, they are necessarily good. For example, God has provided a spouse to meet the needs of companionship. God has provided a place of employment as a means for meeting the needs of the family. God provides food and drink to sustain our bodies. But God has also designed the universe in a particular way so that there is an order to the things that we should love.

Because God made specific objects to meet specific needs, we will ultimately not be satisfied when we seek to substitute one good for another. Hence, Naugle warns that we should love "God, people, animals, places, and things the way God, people, animals, places, and things should be love. Nothing but frustration lies ahead if this order is reversed."[18] If the loves are ordered, then one must be highest. One love should be above all other loves.

Revealed in Scripture

While one's worldview and culture may influence one's understanding of right purpose, ultimately, Scripture reveals God's position on the topic. "What is the chief end? What is the highest good?

To Seek the Kingdom of God

Certainly, anything that Scripture commands is good. Hence, Jesus's command to go into all of the world and make disciples is good (Matt. 28:18 - 20). Similarly, Paul's admonition to "pray without ceasing" (1 Thess. 5:16 - 18) or speaking the truth in love (Eph. 4:15) are good. These examples represent behaviors that God blesses. But the question that most interests us is that which captured Aristotle: Is there one good that we should pursue above all other goods?

A quick survey of the behaviors that seem to capture the lives of our neighbors and co-workers may suggest that the greatest good – that which should receive most of our attention and effort – involves worldly pursuits. Hence, we are not surprised that the majority of people appear overly preoccupied with what they will eat, how they will pay their bills, and who they should marry. Against these normal concerns, however, Jesus commanded his disciples to "seek first the kingdom of God and his righteousness" (Matt. 6:33).[19]

Meaning of the Kingdom

What is the meaning of the phrase, "kingdom of God?" In various passages, biblical writers use the phrase "kingdom of God" with a future perspective. It is used by the biblical authors to contrast characteristics of this age with the characteristics of the Age to Come (e.g., Mk. 10:30; Matt. 12:32). In this sense, the "Age to Come" is synonymous with the Kingdom of God. We see this contrast in parables, such as the parable of the wheat and the weeds (Matt. 13:36-43) and the parable of the soils (Matt. 13:19). In these two parables, we see that in the Age to Come, God will separate the righteous from the wicked. The unrighteous, if you will, will not enter into this kingdom.[20] The kingdom of God, therefore, refers to that future kingdom when God will exercise his sovereignty over all the earth.

Other biblical passages also allude to this future aspect of the kingdom. In the sixth discourse of his gospel, Matthew records Jesus' conversation with his disciples about last things. The entire discourse, which includes the "gospel of the kingdom" clearly points to a future eschatological kingdom (Matt. 24:14). Similarly, Jesus' model prayer includes the petition that God's kingdom might come and that his will be done (Matt. 6:9-12).[21]

As we have described it, the kingdom of God has an eschatological emphasis – a time when God reigns over all of his kingdom. However, the kingdom of God also has a present sense. Matthew, for instance, describes the incarnation of Jesus as inaugurating the kingdom (Matt. 3:2), and Jesus himself hints that the beginning of his ministry in some fashion fulfills Old Testament prophesy about the kingdom (Lk. 4:21; c.f., Mk.1:14-15). When the Pharisees questioned Jesus about the timing of the kingdom, Jesus responded: "Look, here it is. Behold, the kingdom of God is in your midst" (Lk. 17:20). Likewise, Jesus accents the present aspect of the kingdom with respect to his ability to exorcise evil spirits. "But if it is by the Spirit of God that I cast out demons, then the kingdom of God has come upon you" (Matt. 12:28).

Whether the emphasis is on the present or the future, the basic thrust of the term kingdom refers to God's activity of reigning; it emphasizes

God's rule or sovereignty.[22] Thus, Ladd rightly notes that the future eschaton had not arrived with Christ's ministry, but rather, God's kingdom rule and power were being displayed.[23]

Importance of the Kingdom

Most commentators recognize the centrality of the kingdom in Jesus' teaching and ministry. Biblical author R.E.O. White writes:

> The kingdom of God is the central theme in the teaching of Jesus, and his unique contribution to ethical thought. The sovereignty of God, the absolute- ness of the divine law, the inescapable will of God, or all he related to the finality of moral obligation, the certainty that right and good will be vindicated, the faith that the king of all your loves man and seeks his welfare.[24]

Similarly, New Testament author G.E. Ladd notes: "Modern scholarship is quite unanimous in the opinion that the kingdom of God was the central message of Jesus."[25] This centrality is seen in Jesus' Sermon on the Mount (Matt. 5-7).

Character of the Kingdom

Lay people and scholars alike often refer to the first part of the Sermon as the "Beatitudes," from the Latin word for "blessed": *beatus*. Although some Bibles translate it as "happy," I think this translation falls short of the intended meaning. To be blessed by God means to receive God's approval. These are the traits which God approves, and consequently, he blesses. The first and the last beatitude receive the same reward: "theirs is the kingdom of heaven" (5:3, 10). From an interpretive standpoint, this bracketing forms what we call an "inclusion." As a result, the six beatitudes between these brackets are included in the same theme – character traits and actions that receive God's blessings. Because these attitudes and character traits are associated with God's blessings, they are by definition morally good. Moreover, these morally good traits are further linked to the kingdom of God.

Jesus outlines eight traits that characterize the citizens of his kingdom. They include being "poor in spirit" (5:3), "mourn" (5:4), "gentle" (5:5), "hungering and thirsting for righteousness" (5:6), "merciful" (5:7), "pureness in heart" (5:8), "peacemaking" (5:9), and "being persecuted" (5:10). In these traits, Jesus is not speaking generally of those who are poor, or hungry, or thirsty. To the contrary, his subject is kingdom traits. Consequently, the kind of poor that receives God's approval is that which recognizes its spiritual bankruptcy before God, even to the degree of mourning over it. The kind of hunger and thirsting that God approves seeks his righteousness — it seeks to conform to his will. Moreover, those who possess these traits not only receive God's approval (his blessing), but in particular, one receives a series of rewards: comfort (5:4), an inheritance (5:5), and satisfaction (5:6). To the watching world —citizens of this world — these are not traits (like poor in spirit) to be desired. Indeed, "the things of God are foolishness to man;" but if we seek the approval of God rather than man, then these attitudes will speak to our hearts and receive our deepest attention.

Jesus makes clear that these character traits are not to be practiced only in private. To be sure, they constitute a major aspect of our witness to the world. Consequently, we may be persecuted, as the last beatitude claims. More importantly, however, our response to this persecution affords us the opportunity to exercise significant influence on society. Jesus illustrates this influence with two metaphors: salt and light. "You are the salt of the earth" (5:13). "You are the light of the world" (5:14). By living in a manner that conforms to kingdom character traits, we cannot help but influence society for the good. Like salt, we delay the world's moral and spiritual putrefaction. Like a light in a dark room, our actions will not be hidden. Rather, "they will see your good works and glorify your father who is in heaven" (5:16). Peter draws the same conclusion in his epistle: "Keep your behavior excellent among the Gentiles, so that on . . . on account of your good deeds, as they observe them, they glorify God" (1 Ptr. 2:12). When we live as citizens of the kingdom of God, we not only receive God's approval with present and future rewards, but we also influence others to glorify God.

Righteousness of the Kingdom

What we have said is that Jesus advocates a certain kind of character for the citizens of God's kingdom. He described conformity to this way of living in verse six as "righteousness," and states in this section that "unless your righteousness surpasses that of the scribes and Pharisees, you shall not enter the kingdom of heaven" (5:20). It appears, therefore, that Jesus is teaching a new kind of righteousness – a Kingdom ethic. And to some degree he is. It is perhaps a different ethic from that which was taught by the scribes and rabbis. But he goes to great pains to demonstrate that it was not a different ethic from that which the prophets of old had taught. It was simply different from the world's ethic.

• Right Heart Produces Right Conduct: To be sure, Jesus' Kingdom ethic was in harmony with the teachings of the Old Testament prophets. Jesus says, "Do not think that I have come to abolish the Law and the Prophets; I did not come to abolish, but to fulfill" (5:17). To emphasize his commitment to the Law, he adds, "not the smallest letter or stroke shall pass away from the Law until it is accomplished" (5:18). However, Jesus cannot assume that what the listeners had been taught agreed with the Law. To be sure, the rabbis had added tradition to the Law.

• Right Conduct Springs from a Right Heart: The rabbis emphasized outward conformity to the law, but Jesus taught that obedience included both the outward action and the inward disposition. Kingdom ethics included right conduct and right heart. Accordingly, Jesus gives six examples from the Law, introducing each with the phrase "you have heard it said."

The scribes and the Pharisees had taught the people that the Law demanded:

1. "You shall not murder" (5:21)
2. "You shall not commit adultery" (5:27);
3. "Whoever divorces his wife" (5:31);
4. "You shall not make false vows" (5:33);
5. "An eye for an eye" (5:38); and
6. "Love your neighbor" (5:43).

Kingdom ethics does not reject outward conformity to these laws. But Jesus taught that the Law itself demanded more than outward conformity. The Law addressed even the attitudes that gave rise to those actions.

1. Thus, not just murder, but anger violated the Law (5:22);
2. Not just adultery, but lust (5:28);
3. The Law not only commanded love of neighbor, but love for the enemy (5:44).
4. In short, Jesus taught that obedience to the Law ultimately required being "perfect as your heavenly Father is perfect" (5:48).

In outlining this section, you will notice that Jesus' teaching illustrated two of the major parts of a moral event – right conduct and right heart. As kingdom citizens, Jesus makes clear that God blesses behavior (e.g., not murder, not adultery, not stealing) only when those behaviors arise from a pure heart. The heart, for Jesus, was as important as the behavior, primarily because the heart strongly influences the behavior.

• Right Conduct and Right Heart Spring from a Right Purpose: Jesus has just emphasized that the righteousness of the kingdom begins with the heart; nevertheless, it is still involves an outward component. And having exhorted his followers to perfection, he knows of humanity's propensity to sin. That is, in our attempt to live piously, our motives become adulterated, and we exchange the glory of God for its lesser cousin, the praise of men. Consequently, he issues this warning: "Beware of practicing your righteousness before men" (6:1). The warning is that we would try to live before men rather than God – that we would seek the approval of our neighbor rather than the blessing from God. In this regard, Jesus has moved to the third part of a moral event – right purpose. If our behavior has as its goal the praise of men, then it still results in God's disapproval. Four different times Jesus says that when we seek the approval of men, "they have their reward in full" (6:1, 2, 5, 16). In other words, that is all the reward we get. It cancels out any reward from God. As a result, "you have no reward with your Father in heaven" (6:1).

Then Jesus goes on to give three examples of worship where believers can practice their righteousness before men instead of God. In each example, Jesus likens the actions to those of the "hypocrites." Secondly, he states again that the only reward received is the acclamation of the world. And lastly, he describes what the practice would look like if it were performed in true righteousness: charitable giving (6:2-4), prayer (6:5-15), and fasting (6:6-18).

Interestingly, this point illustrates for us the third component of a moral event: the right purpose. When Jesus said that the righteousness of his disciples must surpass that of the Pharisees, he was speaking about the heart of the moral agent. In this section when Jesus warns about practicing one's righteousness before men (6:1), he is speaking to the goal or purpose of ethical behavior. In other words, if one performs the right conduct (e.g., giving alms to the poor) in an effort to please others, then one receives only the praise of others and not the praise (i.e., blessings) of God. In fact, the heart again appears to be determinative. When one is selfish (the heart), one may seek the praise of others rather than God (right purpose).

Perspective of the Kingdom

In the previous section and verses, Jesus argued somewhat negatively regarding the practice of righteousness in the kingdom: it should not be like the Pharisees and the hypocrites. In this section, he begins to lay out more positively what the proper perspective ought to be for those who are citizens of the kingdom of God. Kingdom living is not just about giving in a way that is non-hypocritical; it not just about loving your neighbor; in short, it involves far more than successfully wading through one issue after another. It involves the Christian's entire perspective. To that end, Jesus lays two overarching perspectives that should guide the Christian: undivided devotion and unwavering trust.

Positively, Jesus implores his disciples to "lay up for yourselves treasures in heaven, where neither moth nor rust destroys, and where thieves do not break in or steal" (6:20). The treasures Christ has in mind, or course, result in God's approval – "blessed is the man." Hence, these treasures are ethically good. In this verse, Jesus is not condemning wealth. Rather, he is asking for an undivided devotion to God's kingdom. There is nothing wrong with monetary, or political, or even occupational success. Having nice or expensive things are not evil in and of themselves. However, these treasures become morally wrong when our focus shifts from the kingdom to the treasure. Why? "For where your treasure is, there your heart will be also" (6:21). We can become so possessed with the things of this world, that God's kingdom and his will get pushed aside. As Jesus states later, we become "slaves" to a different master (6:24). He calls us, however, to be "devoted to one" (6:24).

The second overarching perspective for kingdom citizens is unwavering trust. The argument goes like this. Because earthly treasures do not ultimately satisfy (6:19-21), and because I must choose between God and money (6:24), I should not worry about mere things. The "mere things" to which I am referring Jesus called "what you eat and drink" (6:25). In the present passage, the *a fortiori* argument is implicit. It goes like this: If God provides us with life and bodies (greater things), then how much more will he not also provide us with food and clothes (lesser things)?

If we worry about the things of this world – what we eat or what we wear – does this not imply that we are pursuing the same things that materialists and "non-citizens" are pursuing? Our worry implies that our devotion is not to the kingdom, but to this world and its treasures. Secondly, our worry about the things of this world also suggests a lack of trust in the God. We say that "our Father knows all things," (6:8) and yet we do not trust him with these "lesser" things. Our conduct is an advertisement to the world that we do not trust God. Consequently, Jesus concludes, "Seek first his kingdom and his righteousness, and all these things shall be added to you" (6:33). Citizens of God's kingdom should seek his kingdom and seek his righteousness, and trust that God will provide enough to cover their needs. As kingdom citizens, these overarching ideas – undivided devotion and unwavering trust – guide our entire perspective in this life. In his model prayer, in fact, Jesus exhorts his followers to pray that the kingdom would come and that God's will would be accomplished on earth as it is in heaven (Matt. 6:9-10).

Thus, the kingdom is not just good; it is of first importance. Kingdom-living, which includes the heart as well as the action, is lived before God and neighbor. And when it is lived consistently and our life's priorities are characterized by kingdom-seeking, we reflect God's rule in our own life before the watching world. When we are kingdom-seeking citizens, we "image" God, and this attitude and behavior brings glory to God.

> **Exercise 4.3**: The business world is more often than not thought of in terms of "cut-throat" and climbing the corporate ladder of success. List various character traits, behaviors, and purposes that capture this common understanding of the business environment. Contrast these characteristics with the traits, behaviors, and purposes of one who should be pursuing a Kingdom ethic. ∎

To Glorify God

What we have been arguing in this chapter is that there exists a highest good for which all Christians should strive. Moreover, Jesus indicated that this highest good involved seeking first his kingdom and his righteousness. How does this goal, however, compare to the supreme purpose set forth in the Westminster Shorter Catechism? The Shorter Catechism asks the question, "What is the chief end of man?" The Shorter Catechism's answer to the question is, "Man's chief end is to glorify God, and to enjoy him forever."

According to the catechism, therefore, the highest good is God's glory. Certainly, Scripture agrees with the catechism's conclusion. In his *An Introduction of Biblical Ethics*, Jones outlines how God's glory is seen through God's own redemptive work through history.

> For example, Scripture notes God created the world for his glory (Prov 16:4; Col 1:16-18); got elected his people before the foundation of the world for his own glory (Eph. 1:5-6); God created man for his own glory (Isa. 49:3); God delivered Israel from Egypt for his own glory(Ps. 106:7-8); God restored Israel

after their exile for his own glory (Isa. 48:9-11); God sent his son into the world that Gentiles might glorify him for his mercy (Rom 15:8-9); God sent the Holy Spirit to glorify his Son (John 16:14); God commands his people to do all things for his own glory (1Cor. 10:31; 1 Peter 4:11).[26]

Meaning of the Glory of God

The Hebrew word (kabod) from which the term glory derives signifies "weighty" and it came to refer to anything that possessed the qualities of excellence or splendor.[27] Because God is excellent and praiseworthy, the term eventually came to refer to the revelation of God.[28] In his classic text, *Desiring God*, author and theologian John Piper beautifully captures this aspect of glory.

> God's glory is the beauty of his manifold perfections. It can refer to the bright and awesome radiance that sometimes breaks forth in visible manifestations. Or it can refer to the infinite moral excellence of his character. In either case it signifies a reality of infinite greatness and worth.[29]

In the New Testament period, the Greek word *doxa* provides the root from which the term glory arises. Similar to its use in the Old Testament, glory connoted the visible presence of God. In addition, however, it came to refer to the response of individuals to God's glory; it connotes "ascribing glory."[30]

Because glory is associated with God's revelation, it may be ascribed to creation. "The heavens declare the glory of God" (Ps. 19:1). Because humans are created in God's image, we too reflect his glory (1 Cor. 11:7). However, in the second sense of the New Testament usage, humans reflect God's glory – we glorify God – when we consciously respond to him. Because God lacks nothing, we are not technically "giving" him anything. We are ascribing him glory. In this regard, glory is a behavior and a choice.[31] Consequently, we are commanded to glorify God in all that we do (1 Cor. 10:31).

Significance of the Glory of God

If everything we do – eat, drink, or whatever – is for God's glory, then seeking first the kingdom of God is also for his glory. And it is not difficult to see how these two ideas are related. God is sovereign and rules over all creation. This truth is not doubted. Nevertheless, there remains outposts where God's rule is not recognized. As citizens of God's kingdom, we seek first and foremost what is best for the kingdom.[32] This seeking may be accomplished through various means, such as expanding God's rule through evangelism, promoting justice, and performing acts of mercy and kindness. When we do these things, God will be glorified and we will obtain our greatest happiness. We will have sought the kingdom, glorified God, and achieved our *summum bonum*.

Exercise 4.4: From the opening story of the chapter about Henry Kaestner, can you identify portions of the narrative that point to his purpose in Bandwidth.com? Did his purpose at Bandwidth.com illustrate seeking first the kingdom of God and God's glory? ■

Exercise 4.5: Go to the webpage for Praxislabs.org. Compare and contrast their idea of redemptive entrepreneurship with what we have described as right purpose? Visit the webpage for sovereignscapital.com? According to what is found on the company's website, would you say that the company meets the criteria for redemptive entrepreneurship? ■

Summary

In this chapter, we have addressed the third major component of morality: a right purpose. By tracing the history of philosophical and ethical thinking of the two major philosophical camps (Naturalism and Idealism), we showed everyone is seeking a life of happiness or blessedness – a life that is flourishing. This purpose in life is true for everyone. What differs between practitioners of the different philosophies is how they define this happiness. Ultimately, one's highest purpose is influenced by one's worldview and one's culture.

For Christians, however, this highest purpose – *summum bonum* – is revealed in Scripture. This purpose is characterized by seeking first God's kingdom and his glory. In fact, by seeking first God's kingdom, one is glorifying God and thus, seeking the highest purpose.

Chapter 5: Summary of Ethical Methodology

Right Heart

Situated in the Doctrine of Sanctification

When we began this study, we noted that any study of business ethics must recognize that the ethical life itself – the Christian life – begins with the work of God. Consequently, we situated the study of ethics within the doctrine of sanctification. Our ability and our desire to live the Christian life begins with God's decision to set us apart, to sanctify us. As we stated earlier, this "setting apart" occurs at the moment of salvation when God sets us apart to live differently than the rest of the world. However, our ability to live successfully as ones who are set apart is a challenge because of the depths of our depravity. Consequently, through the sanctification process God molds us into the image of his Son, Jesus Christ. We are becoming more like him.

Described by Particular Character Traits

Throughout various facets of our study, we have noted the character traits of those who have been "set apart" – sanctified. We have described it as those who are committed to moral excellence, committed to faithfully fulfilling their family responsibilities, committed to self-control, to service, and to integrity (1 Tim. 3:1-7). We have likened it to having the fruits of the spirit evident within one's life: love, joy, peace, patience, kindness, goodness, faithfulness, gentleness, and self-control (Gal. 5:22-23). In our survey of the Sermon on the Mount, Jesus further illustrated that these character traits of kingdom citizens included being "poor in spirit," "hungering and thirsting for righteousness," possessing a "pureness of heart" (Matt. 5:3-10).

Equated with Who We Are

These character traits are important because they signify largely who we are as individuals. We are not simply people who do kind things, we are kind people. We are not simply people who at times exhibit peace and patience, but rather, we are peaceful and patient people. In this study, we have used the phrase "right heart" to denote this kind of character. Thus, when I speak of the heart, I am referring not just of who we are as individuals, but to how God fundamentally sees us as individuals.

In his Sermon on the Mount, Jesus highlights the importance of the heart for living rightly. While he was concerned with righteous behavior – not taking innocent life, faithfulness to one's spouse, in speaking the truth – he was equally concerned with the attitude and disposition of one's heart. For the attitudes of one's heart – lust, anger, wrath, greed – give rise to certain current behaviors (Matt. 5:21 – 42). In another passage, Jesus teaches the same point: "the good person out of the good treasure of his heart produces good, and that evil person out of the evil treasure produces evil, for out of the abundance of the heart his mouth speaks" (Luke 6:45).

Consequently, right conduct begins with a right heart: who we are as individuals. While it is true that all of our actions are a window into our heart, it also true that our actions reflect the degree to which God's sanctifying process has taken hold in our lives. When confronted with a moral question, one must take considerable care that his decisions to act a certain way flow from a heart that is pure. One way that is helpful in this situation is to ask the following questions: "Am I acting in a way that demonstrates my love for God and love for my neighbor?"

Right Purpose

Arises from a Right Heart

If one has been set apart by God and has experienced considerable progress in the sanctifying process, then one has begun to move from seeking one's own pleasure to seeking those things which most glorify God. To be sure, this becomes the Christian's *summum bonum*. In our discussion of the right purpose in business ethics, we referred to this as the teleological component. It refers to the ultimate goal or purpose for our actions.

A person engaged in business affairs may be pursuing any number of good purposes. For example, one may be in a service industry where the services one's company provides truly benefits the lives of its customers; the individuals are demonstrably better off. For several years, I worked as a professional tax accountant at a public accounting firm in Dallas, Texas. As a result of my accounting work, I earned a salary that helped to provide for my family's needs. In addition, I sincerely helped numerous individuals not only to stay in a state of good standing with proper government authorities (Secretary of State, IRS, etc.), but to actually be in a better position financially; my work benefitted them personally. I helped some to avoid bankruptcy; I helped some to maximize the amount of funds that they could bequeath to their children. I helped my clients make financial decisions that strengthened their company financially, as well as them individually.

Seeks God's Kingdom and His Glory

As an accountant, therefore, I had various legitimate goals, goals which could rightly be characterized as good. Certainly, making a salary and providing for my family were important. And, providing valuable services to my clients was important to me and to the company for which I worked. Even though many of these goals were good, they were not of ultimate importance. Rather, my ultimate goal was extending God's rule into this world in which I lived so that he might be glorified. As image bearers, we are the hands and the feet of Christ in this fallen world. And in whatever work we find ourselves, we are to use the resources that God has given us – mental capacity, opportunity, capital, etc. – for good. It is work that touches the lives of everyone around us and is perhaps characterized by Isaiah's prophecy of "binding up the brokenhearted, proclaiming freedom to the captives, and release from darkness for the prisoners" (Isa. 61).

Many of our goals in business are not bad in and of themselves: profit, growth, service, etc. Indeed, they are good! Nevertheless, these good goals can become bad when they become an end unto themselves rather than a means to a greater goal: God's kingdom and his glory. Hence, Jesus warns his followers to "seek first the kingdom of God and his righteousness" (Matt. 6:33). When confronted with a moral question, one must take considerable care to ensure that they are behaving in a manner consistent with a right purpose. One way that is helpful in the situation is to ask the following question: "Am I acting in a way that demonstrates that I am pursuing the kingdom of God and his glory?"

Right Conduct

Inter-related to the Three Parts of Morality

In this text, we have been discussing the importance of the three parts of morality. In this final section, were hoping to emphasize the inter-relatedness of the three parts. We have already seen how one's heart relates to one's purpose. Having been set apart by God, that which is most important to one's life changes. God's kingdom in God's glory becomes the ultimate goal. In a similar way, conduct is also related to one's heart and purpose. Again, Jesus' discussion of the kingdom in the Sermon on the Mount beautifully illustrates this point. Jesus warned about practicing one's righteousness before others (Matt. 6:1). The warning is this: if we tried to live our life before men rather than God, then the approval of others is all we will receive and not the blessings of God. When our goal is directed toward God's glory, our good conduct receives God's approval – his blessing.

Obeys God's Moral Standards and Imitates God's Character

Scripture identifies another way that character and conduct are related. We stated earlier that an important way to identify the character of our heart is to ask whether or not we were operating from a desire to love God and love our neighbor. John the evangelist records the words of Jesus teaching his disciples: "The one who has my commands and keeps them is the one who loves me" (John 14:21). Thus, Jesus connects our love for God – our heart – with obedience to his commands. While our discussion on right conduct centered on one's duty to obey God's law and imitate God's character, the present discussion demonstrates one's obedience to these duties flows from a right heart.

When confronted with a moral question, one must take considerable care to ensure that one's behavior is consistent with one's character and goal. One helpful way to ensure the situation is to ask the following question: "Am I acting in a way that is consistent with God's moral standards and God's moral character?"

Bibliography

Christian Spirituality: Five Views on Sanctification. edited by Donald L. Alexander: IVP Academic, 1988.

Abelson, J. *The Immanence of God.* Macmillan, 1912.

Allen, Michael. *Sanctification.* edited by Michael Allen and Scott R. Swain. Grand Rapids: Zondervan, 2017.

Aquinas, Thomas. *Summa Theologica.* Translated by Fathers of the english Dominican Province. New York: Benziger Brothers, 1911 - 1925.

Aristotle. "Nichomachean Ethics." In *The Basic Works of Aristotle.*, edited by Richard McKeoon, 935-1126: Random House, 1941.

Augustine. *Concerning the Nature of the Good.* edited by Whitney J. Oates: Random House, 1948.

Augustine. *The City of God.* Vol. 4. Grand Rapids: Eerdmans, 1973.

Augustine. *Of the Morals of the Catholic Church.* edited by Philip Schaff. Peabody, MA: Hendrickson Publishers, 1994.

Augustine. *Enchiridion on Faith, Hope and Love.* Regnery, 1996.

Baillie, John. *Our Knowledge of God.* London: Oxford University Press, 1939.

Baird, James Douglas. "Analogical Knowledge: A Systematic Interpretation of Cornelius Van Til's Theological Epistemology." *Mid-America Journal of Theology* 26, no. 3 (2015): 77-103.

Barth, Karl. *Church Dogmatics: Doctrine of the Word of God.* Vol. III, edited by G. W. Bromiley and Thomas F. Torrance. Edinburgh: T&T Clark, 1956.

Barth, Karl. *Church Dogmatics: Doctrine of the Word of God.* Vol. 1. Edinburgh: T&T Clark, 1956.

Bentham, Jeremy. *An Introduction to the Principles of Morals and Legislation.* London: Clarendon Press, 1892.

Bivens, Josh, Lora Engdahl, Elise Gould, Teresa Koreger, Celine McNicholas, Lawrence Mishel, Zane Mokhiber, Heidi Shierholz, Marni von Wilpert, and Ben Zipperer. "How Today's Unions Help Working People." Economic Policy Institute. Last modified August 24, 2017, 2017. Accessed November 9, 2019, 2019.

Boatright, John R. "Fiduciary Duties and the Shareholder-Management Relation: Or, What's So Special About Shareholders?" *Business Ethics Quarterly* (1994): 393-407.

Boatright, John R. *Ethics and the Conduct of Business.* 7 ed. NJ: Pearson, 2012.

Bowen, Howard R and F Ernest Johnson. *Social Responsibility of the Businessman.* New York: Harper, 1953.

Bridges, Jerry. *The Discipline of Grace: God's Role and Our Role in the Pursuit of Holiness.* Colorado: Navpress, 1994.

Brunner, Emil. *The Devine Imperative.* Louisville: Westminster Press, 1947.

Bunyan, John. *The Pilgrim's Progress.* Edited by Charles W. Elliot: P.F. Collier & Son, 1909.

Cafferky, Michael E. *Business Ethics in Biblical Perspective: A Comprehensive Introduction.* Downers Grove: InterVarsity Press, 2015.

Carnell, Eward J. *The Case for Biblical Christianity.* Grand Rapids: Eerdmans, 1969.

Carnell, John. *An Introduction to Christian Apologetics.* Grand Rapids: Eerdmans, 1948.

Carroll, Archie B. "A Three-Dimensional Conceptual Model of Corporate Performance." *Academy of Management Review* 4, no. 4 (1979): 497-505.

Carroll, Archie B. "Corporate Social Responsibility: Evolution of a Definitional Construct." *Business & society* 38, no. 3 (1999): 268-95.

Chapell, Bryan. *Holiness by Grace:: Delighting in the Joy Tha Tis Our Strenghth.* Wheaton: Crossway, 2001.

Chewning, Richard C., ed. *Biblical Principles & Business: The Foundations,* Christians in the Marketplace. Colorado: Navpress, 1989.

Chewning, Richard C., ed. *Biblical Principles & Economics: The Foundations,* Christians in the Marketplace. Colorado: Navpress, 1989.

Chewning, Richard C., ed. *Biblical Principles & Business: The Practice,* Christians in the Marketplace. Colorado: Navpress, 1990.

Chewning, Richard C., John W. Eby, and Sirley J. Roels. *Business through the Eyes of Faith.* San Francisco: Harper & Row, 1990.

Chilton, Bruce and J. I. H. McDonald. *Jesus and the Ethics of the Kingdom.* Grand Rapids: Eerdmans, 1987.

Clark, Gordon H. "The Bible as Truth." *Bibliotheca Sacra* 114 (1957): 157-70.

Cochran, Philip L and Robert A Wood. "Corporate Social Responsibility and Financial Performance." *Academy of Management Journal* 27, no. 1 (1984): 42-56.

Cowper, William. *The Winter Walk at Noon.* Ward, Lock, & Co., Warwick House, 1882.

Craig, William Lane. *Reasonable Faith: Christian Truth and Apologetics.* Wheaton: Crossway, 2008.

Crenshaw, Ben. *The Moral Argument against the Minimum Wage.* 2015.

Curran, Charles E. *The Catholic Moral Tradition Today: A Synthesis.* Washington, D.C.: Georgetown University, 1999.

Dagg, John Leadley. *Manual of Theology.* Vol. 1. Nashville: Southern Baptist Publication Society, 1859.

Dalman, Gustaf. *The Words of Jesus.* Edinburgh: T & T Clark, 1902.

Davis, Keith. "Can Business Afford to Ignore Social Responsibilities?" *California Management Review* 2, no. 3 (1960): 70-76.

Davis, Keith and Robert Lowell Blomstrom. *Business and Its Environment.* McGraw-Hill, 1966.

de Graff, Graeme. *God and Morality.* edited by Ian T. Ramsey. London: SCM Press, 1973.

Dieter, Melvin, Anthony Hoekema, Stanley M. Horton, McQuilkin, and John F. Walvoord. *Five Views on Sanctification.* Grand Rapids: Zondervan, 1987.

Dodd, C. H. *The Parables of the Kingdom.* Nisbet, 1941.

Douma, Jochem. *Responsible Conduct: Principles Ofchristian Ethics. Translated by Nelson D.* 2003.

Drucker, Peter F. "Converting Social Problems into Business Opportunities: The New Meaning of Corporate Social Responsibility." *California Management Review (pre-1986)* 26, no. 000002 (1984): 53.

Edwards, Jonathan. *Christian Love and Its Fruits.* Sovereign Grace Publishers, 1971.

Erickson, Millard J. *Christian Theology.* Grand Rapids, MI: Baker Academic, 1998.

Evan, William M and R Edward Freeman. "A Stakeholder Theory of the Modern Corporation: Kantian Capitalism." In *Ethical Theory and Business,* edited by T. Beauchamp and N. Bowie, 75-93. Englewood Cliffs: Prentice Hall, 1988.

Fletcher, Joseph F. *Situation Ethics: The New Morality.* Louisville: Westminster John Knox Press, 1966.

Foster, Richard J., Emilie Griffin, and others. *Spiritual Classics: Selected Readings on the Twelve Spiritual Disciplines.* New York: Harper Collins, 2000.

Frame, John M. *The Doctrine of the Christian Life: A Theology of Lordship*. Phillipsburg: P&R Publishing, 2008.

Frederick, William C. "The Growing Concern over Business Responsibility." *California Management Review* 2, no. 4 (1960): 54-61.

Freeman, R Edward. "The Politics of Stakeholder Theory: Some Future Directions." *Business Ethics Quarterly* (1994): 409-21.

Freeman, R Edward. *Strategic Management: A Stakeholder Approach*. Cambridge: Cambridge university press, 2010. Originally published as 1984.

Geisler, Norman L. *Christian Ethics: Contemporary Issues and Options*. Grand Rapids, MI: Baker Academic, 2010.

George, Robert P. *Making Men Moral: Civil Liberties and Public Morality*. Oxford: Clarendon Press, 1995.

Goodpaster, Kenneth E. "Ethical Imperatives and Corporate Leadership." *The Ruffin Series in Business Ethics* (1991): 89-110.

Grenz, Stanley J. *The Moral Quest: Foundations of Christian Ethics*. Downers Grove: InterVarsity Press, 2000.

Grenz, Stanley J. *The Moral Quest: Foundations of Christian Ethics*. Downers Grove: InterVarsity Press, 1997.

Grudem, Wayne. *Business for the Glory of God: The Bible's Teaching on the Moral Goodness of Business*. Wheaton: Crossway, 2003.

Grudem, Wayne A. *Systematic Theology: An Introduction to Biblical Doctrine*. Grand Rapids: Zondervan, 2009.

Gushee, David P. and Glen H. Stassen. *Kingdom Ethics: Following Jesus in Contemporary Context*. Grand Rapids: Eerdmans, 2016.

Gutherie, Donald. *New Testament Theology*. Downers Grove: InterVarsity Press, 1981.

Hare, John E. *God and Morality: A Philosophical History*. Hoboken, NJ: Wiley-Blackwell, 2009.

Hare, John E. *God's Command.* London: Oxford University Press, 2015.

Harrington, Daniel J. and Keenan James F. *Paul and Virtue Ethics: Building Bridges between New Testament Studies and Moral Theology.* Lanham, MD: Rowman & Littlefield Publishers, 2010.

Harris, Michael J. *Divine Command Ethics: Jewish and Christian Perspectives.* Abingdon: Routledge, 2004.

Hauerwas, Stanley. *Truthfulness and Tragedy.* Notre Dame, IN: University of Notre Dame Press, 1977.

Hauerwas, Stanley. *The Community of Character.* Notre Dame, IN: University of Notre Dame Press, 1981.

Hauerwas, Stanley. *Peaceable Kingdom: A Primer in Christian Ethics.* Notre Dame, IN: University of Notre Dame Press, 1983.

Hauerwas, Stanley. *Vision and Virtue: Essays in Christian Ethical Reflection.* Notre Dame: Fides Publishers, 1986.

Hauerwas, Stanley. *The Peaceable Kingdom: A Primer in Christian Ethics.* Notre Dame, IN: University of Notre Dame Pess, 1991.

Haverwas, Stanley. *A Community of Character.* Notre Dame, IN: University of Notre Dame Press Notre Dame, 1981.

Hawtrey, Ralph. G. *The Economic Problem.* London: Longmans & Co., 1926.

Heermance, Edgar L. *The Ethics of Business: A Study of Current Standards.* New York: Harper & Brothers, 1927.

Henry, Carl F. H. *Christian Personal Ethics.* Grand Rapids: Eerdmans, 1957.

Henry, Carl F. H. "God Who Speaks and Shows." In *God, Revelation, and Authority.* , vol 2. Waco, TX: Word Books, 1999.

Henry, Carl F. H. "God Who Speaks and Shows: Fifteen Theses, Part Two." In *God, Revelation, and Authority.* , vol 3. Waco, TX: Word Books, 1999.

Hill, Alexander. *Just Business: Christian Ethics for the Marketplace.* Downers Grove, IL: Intervarsity, 1997.

Hoffecker, W. Andrew and G. K. Beale. "Biblical Epistemology: Revelation." In *Building a Christian Worldview*, edited by W. Andrew Holffeker and Gary Scott Smith, 193-216. Phillipsburg, NJ: P&R, 1986.

Jones, David Clyde. *Biblical Christian Ethics*. Grand Rapids, MI: Baker Books, 1994.

Jones, David W. *An Introduction to Biblical Ethics*. Nashville, TN: B&H Academic, 2013.

Kant, Immanuel. *Groundwork of Metaphysic of Morals*. edited by Allen W. Wood. New Haven: Yale University Press, 2002.

Kant, Immanuel. *Fundamental Principles of the Metaphysics of Morals*. Dover Publications, 2005.

Kant, Immanuel. *Religion within the Bounds of Bare Reason*. Hackett Publishing, 2009.

Klonoski, Richard J. "Unapplied Ethics: On the Need for Classical Philosophy in Professional Ethics Education." *Teaching Business Ethics* 7, no. 1 (2003): 21-35.

Kuhn, James and Donald Shriver. *Beyond Success*. New York: Oxford University Press, 1992.

Ladd, George Eldon. *Jesus and the Kingdom: The Eschatology of Biblical Realism*. Harmondsworth: SPCK, 1966.

Ladd, George Eldon. *A Theology of the New Testament*. Grand Rapids: William B. Eerdmans, 1974.

Lewis, C. S. *Mere Christianity*. MacMillan, 1943.

Lind, Dara. "The Ugly History of Racist Policing in America." *Vox Media*. July 7, 2016, 2016, https://www.vox.com/michael-brown-shooting-ferguson-mo/2014/8/19/6031759/ferguson-history-riots-police-brutality-civil-rights.

Long, D. Stephen. *Christian Ethics: A Very Short Introduction*. Vol. 238. London: Oxford University Press, 2010.

Lovin, Robin. *An Introduction to Christian Ethics: Goals, Duties, and Virtues.* Nashville, TN: Abingdon, 2011.

MacIntyre, Alasdair. *After Virtue.* Notre Dame, IN: University of Notre Dave, 1984.

Manson, T. W. *Jesus the Messiah.* Hodder and Stoughton, 1943.

Manson, T. W. *The Teaching of Jesus: Studies of Its Form and Content.* Cambridge: Cambridge University Press, 1959.

McClendon, James William. *Ethics: Systematic Theology.* Vol. 1. Nashville, TN: Abingdon, 1986.

McFayden, Alistair. *The Call to Personhood: A Christian Theory of the Individual in Social Relationships.* Cambridge: Cambridge University Press, 1990.

Moreland, James Porter, James Porter Moreland, and William Lane Craig. *Philosophical Foundations for a Christian Worldview.* Downers Grove: InterVarsity Press, 2003.

Murray, John. *Principles of Conduct: Aspects of Biblical Ethics.* Grand Rapids: Wm. B. Eerdmans, 1957.

Nash, Ronald H. *Life's Ultimate Questions: An Introduction to Philosophy.* Grand Rapids: Zondervan, 1999.

Nassauer, Sarah. "Walmart Takes a Stand on Guns, Gay Rights to Get People to Like It More." *The Wall Street Journal*2018, https://www.wsj.com/articles/walmart-takes-a-stand-on-guns-gay-rights-to-get-people-to-like-it-more-1530805106.

Naugle, David K. *Reordered Love, Reordered Lives.* Grand Rapids: William B. Eerdmans, 2008.

Nelson, Paul. *Narrative and Morality: A Theological Inquiry.* University Park: Pennsylvania State University Press, 1987.

Nielsen, K. *Ethics without God.* Amherst, NY: Prometheus Books, 1990.

O'Donovan, Oliver. *The Desire of the Nations: Rediscovering the Roots of Political Theology*. Cambridge: Cambridge University Press, 1999.

Ornstein, Norm. "The Moral and Economic Imperative to Raise the Minimum Wage." *The Atlantic* (2013).

Owen, John. "The Mortification of Sin: The Necessity, Nature, and Means of It with a Resolution of Various Cases of Conscience Belonging to It." In *The Works of John Owen*, edited by William Goold, vol 6: Johnstone & Hunter, 1850.

Packer, James I. *Fundamentalism and the Word of God: Some Evangelical Principles*. Downers Grove: InterVarsity Fellowship, 1958.

Packer, James I. *God Speaks to Man: Revelation and the Bible*. Louisville: Westminster Press, 1965.

Packer, James I. *God Has Spoken*. Downers Grove, IL: InterVarsity, 1979.

Packer, James I. *Rediscovering Holiness: Know the Fullness of Life with God*. Regal, 2009.

Paliwal, Manisha. *Business Ethics*. New Delhi: New Age International, 2006.

Pascal, Blaise. *Pensées*. Penguin, 1995.

Peterson, David G. *Possessed by God: A New Testament Theology of Sanctification and Holiness*. Vol. 1. Downers Grove: InterVarsity Press, 1995.

Pinches, Charles. "Principle Monism and Action Descriptions: Situationalism and Its Critics Revisited." *Modern Theology* 7, no. 3 (1991): 249-68.

Piper, John. *Desiring God*. Multnomah, 2003.

Plantiga, Alvin. *Two Dozen (or So) Theistic Arguments*. edited by Peter Deane. Cambridge: Cambridge University Press, 2007.

Plato. "Euthyphro." In *Plato: Complete Works*, edited by J. M. Cooper, 1 - 16. Indianapolis, IN: Hackett, 1997.

Pojman, Louis P. *Ethical Theory: Classical and Contemporary Readings*. Belmont, CA: Wadsworth, 1995.

Rae, Scott B. *Moral Choices: An Introduction to Ethics*. New York: Harper Collins, 2009.

Rae, Scott B. and Kenman L. Wong. *Beyond Integrity: A Judeo-Christian Approach to Business Ethics*. Grand Rapids: Zondervan, 2012.

Ramm, B. *Them He Glorified*. Grand Rapids: Eerdmans, 1963.

Reverby, Susan M. *Examining Tuskegee: The Infamous Syphilis Study and Its Legacy*. Chapel Hill: University of North Carolina Press, 2009.

Rossouw, Deon and Leon Van Vuuren. *Business Ethics*. London: Oxford University Press, 2013.

Schaeffer, Francis August. *He Is There and He Is Not Silent*. Carol Stream, IL: Tyndale House Publishers, 1972.

Schweitzer, Albert. *They Mystery of the Kingdom of God: The Secret of Jesus' Messiahship and Passion*. Translated by Walter Lowrie. New York: Dodd, Mead and Company, 1914.

Schweitzer, Albert. *The Quest of the Historical Jesus: A Critical Study of Its Progress from Reimarus to Wrede*. Macmillan, 1964.

Scotus, Duns. *On the Will & Morality*. Translated by William A. Frank. Washington D.C.: Catholic University of America Press, 1997.

Sire, James W. *The Universe Next Door: A Basic Worldview Catalog*. Downers Grove: InterVarsity Press, 2009.

Smith, Adam. *The Wealth of Nations*. Vol. 3. New York: Modern Library, 1776.

Smith, Adam. *The Theory of Moral Sentiments*. Vol. 1759. Oxford University Press, Oxford, edited by D.D. Raphael and A.L. Macfie, 1976.

Sproul, Robert C. *Lifeviews: Make a Christian Impact on Culture and Society*. Grand Rapids: Fleming H. Revell, 1986.

Stigler, George J. "The New Welfare Economics." *The American Economic Review* (1943): 355-59.

Storchevoy, Maxim. *Business Ethics as a Science*. London: Palgrave Macmillan, 2018.

Strobel, Lee. *The Case for a Creator: A Journalist Investigates Scientific Evidence That Points toward God*. Grand Rapids: Zondervan, 2004.

Tarwater, John K. *The Story of the Pentateuch: An Introduction to the Old Testament*. Cedarville: Coram Deo, 2015.

Van Til, Cornelius. *The Protestant Doctrine of Scripture*. Phillipsburg: P&R, 1967.

VanDrunen, David. *A Biblical Case for Natural Law*. Grand Rapids: Acton Institute, 2006.

Weiss, Johannes. *Jesus' Proclamation of the Kingdom of God*. Fortress Press, 1971.

Wells, Samuel and Ben Quash. *Introducing Christian Ethics*. Hoboken, NJ: Wiley-Blackwell, 2010.

White, R. E. O. *Christian Ethics*. Gracewing Publishing, 1994.

Willard, Dallas. *The Spirit of the Disciplines-Reissue: Understanding How God Changes Lives*. Grand Rapids: Zondervan, 1990.

Wolters, Albert M. *Creation Regained: Biblical Basics for a Reformational Worldview*. Grand Rapids: Eerdmans, 1985.

Yadoo, Jordan. "U.S. Labor Unions." Bloomberg. Last modified June 27, 2018, 2018. Accessed November 9, 2019.

Endnotes

Preface

[1] For an example Long's work in introductory Christian ethics, see D. Stephen Long, *Christian Ethics: A Very Short Introduction*, vol. 238 (London: Oxford University Press, 2010).

[2] For examples of the type of things I was taught in courses by Hauerwas and Hays, see Stanley Hauerwas, *Truthfulness and Tragedy* (Notre Dame, IN: University of Notre Dame Press, 1977); Stanley Hauerwas, *The Community of Character* (Notre Dame, IN: University of Notre Dame Press, 1981); Stanley Hauerwas, *Peaceable Kingdom: A Primer in Christian Ethics* (Notre Dame, IN: University of Notre Dame Press, 1983); Stanley Hauerwas, *Vision and Virtue: Essays in Christian Ethical Reflection* (Notre Dame: Fides Publishers, 1986); Stanley Hauerwas, *The Peaceable Kingdom: A Primer in Christian Ethics* (Notre Dame, IN: University of Notre Dame Pess, 1991); Stanley Haverwas, *A Community of Character* (Notre Dame, IN: University of Notre Dame Press Notre Dame, 1981).

[3] Adam Smith, *The Wealth of Nations*, vol. 3 (New York: Modern Library, 1776).

[4] Adam Smith, *The Theory of Moral Sentiments*, vol. 1759, *Oxford University Press, Oxford* (1976).

[5] Ralph. G. Hawtrey, *The Economic Problem* (London: Longmans & Co., 1926), 184.

[6] George J Stigler, "The New Welfare Economics," *The American Economic Review* (1943): 358.

[7] Edgar L Heermance, *The Ethics of Business: A Study of Current Standards* (New York: Harper & Brothers, 1927).

[8] For a good discussion of the history of business ethics, see Maxim Storchevoy, *Business Ethics as a Science* (London: Palgrave Macmillan, 2018), 71-95.

[9] Sample works in this genre include Archie B Carroll, "A Three-Dimensional Conceptual Model of Corporate Performance," *Academy of Management Review* 4, no. 4 (1979); Keith Davis, "Can Business Afford to Ignore Social Responsibilities?," *California Management Review* 2, no. 3 (1960); Keith Davis and Robert Lowell Blomstrom, *Business and Its Environment* (McGraw-Hill, 1966); William C Frederick, "The Growing Concern over Business Responsibility," *California Management Review*

2, no. 4 (1960). For an excellent history of CSR, see Archie B Carroll, "Corporate Social Responsibility: Evolution of a Definitional Construct," *Business & society* 38, no. 3 (1999).

[10] Howard R Bowen and F Ernest Johnson, *Social Responsibility of the Businessman* (New York: Harper, 1953), 6.

[11] See, for example, Philip L Cochran and Robert A Wood, "Corporate Social Responsibility and Financial Performance," *Academy of Management Journal* 27, no. 1 (1984); Peter F Drucker, "Converting Social Problems into Business Opportunities: The New Meaning of Corporate Social Responsibility," *California Management Review (pre-1986)* 26, no. 000002 (1984).

[12] R Edward Freeman, *Strategic Management: A Stakeholder Approach* (Cambridge: Cambridge university press, 2010).

[13] William M Evan and R Edward Freeman, "A Stakeholder Theory of the Modern Corporation: Kantian Capitalism," in *Ethical Theory and Business*, ed. T. Beauchamp and N. Bowie (Englewood Cliffs: Prentice Hall, 1988).

[14] See James Kuhn and Donald Shriver, *Beyond Success* (New York: Oxford University Press, 1992).

[15] Kenneth E Goodpaster, "Ethical Imperatives and Corporate Leadership," *The Ruffin Series in Business Ethics* (1991).

[16] John R Boatright, "Fiduciary Duties and the Shareholder-Management Relation: Or, What's So Special About Shareholders?," *Business Ethics Quarterly* (1994).

[17] See R Edward Freeman, "The Politics of Stakeholder Theory: Some Future Directions," *Business Ethics Quarterly* (1994).

[18] Ibid., 415-18.

[19] Freeman, *Strategic Management: A Stakeholder Approach*.

[20] Freeman, "The Politics of Stakeholder Theory: Some Future Directions."

[21] Manisha Paliwal, *Business Ethics* (New Delhi: New Age International, 2006), 59.

[22] See, for example, John R Boatright, *Ethics and the Conduct of Business*, 7 ed. (NJ: Pearson, 2012); Deon Rossouw and Leon Van Vuuren, *Business Ethics* (London: Oxford University Press, 2013).

[23] Although written from a secular perspective, Richard Klonoski makes a similar argument in an article on "unapplied" ethics. See Richard J Klonoski, "Unapplied Ethics: On the Need for Classical Philosophy in Professional Ethics Education," *Teaching Business Ethics* 7, no. 1 (2003).

[24] Richard C. Chewning, ed. *Biblical Principles & Business: The Foundations*, Christians in the Marketplace (Colorado: Navpress, 1989); Richard C. Chewning, ed. *Biblical Principles & Economics: The Foundations*, Christians in the Marketplace (Colorado: Navpress, 1989); Richard C. Chewning, ed. *Biblical Principles & Business: The Practice*, Christians in the Marketplace (Colorado: Navpress, 1990).

[25] Richard C. Chewning, John W. Eby, and Sirley J. Roels, *Business through the Eyes of Faith* (San Francisco: Harper & Row, 1990).

[26] Alexander Hill, *Just Business: Christian Ethics for the Marketplace* (Downers Grove, IL: Intervarsity, 1997), 13.

[27] Scott B. Rae and Kenman L. Wong, *Beyond Integrity: A Judeo-Christian Approach to Business Ethics* (Grand Rapids: Zondervan, 2012).

Chapter 1

[1] Lee Strobel, *The Case for a Creator: A Journalist Investigates Scientific Evidence That Points toward God* (Grand Rapids: Zondervan, 2004), 34.

[2] Not too long ago, most corporations refrained from entering into debates about social issues. The fear was that such engagement would necessarily disenfranchise a subset of one's customers. Today, this is not the case. Recently, Walmart weighed in on various ethical issues from gun control to gay marriage. Interestingly, they currently espouse positions that just a few years ago would have been unthinkable, especially for a corporation whose headquarters are situated in the deep-south. What this engagement demonstrates is that for a large portion of those engaged in ethical discourse, even from a business perspective, their approach is like choosing one's favorite color: it may shift over time. See Sarah Nassauer, "Walmart Takes a Stand on Guns, Gay Rights to Get People to Like It More," *The Wall Street Journal* 2018, https://www.wsj.com/articles/walmart-takes-a-stand-on-guns-gay-rights-to-get-people-to-like-it-more-1530805106.5106.

[3] Norm Ornstein, "The Moral and Economic Imperative to Raise the Minimum Wage," *The Atlantic* (2013).

[4] Ben Crenshaw, *The Moral Argument against the Minimum Wage* (2015).

[5] We see a similar argument about the power of the Word of God in Mark's gospel. There, Mark argues that the planted word has the potential to grow in massive proportion to its size. The mustard plant is extremely large compared to the mustard seed.

[6] Norman L. Geisler, *Christian Ethics: Contemporary Issues and Options* (Grand Rapids, MI: Baker Academic, 2010), 17.

[7] John Murray, *Principles of Conduct: Aspects of Biblical Ethics* (Grand Rapids: Wm. B. Eerdmans, 1957), 12.

[8] John M. Frame, *The Doctrine of the Christian Life: A Theology of Lordship* (Phillipsburg: P&R Publishing, 2008), 10.

[9] Carl F. H. Henry, *Christian Personal Ethics* (Grand Rapids: Eerdmans, 1957), 16.

[10] I recognize that sometimes it is useful to distinguish them for teaching purposes, such as the distinctions between systematic and practical theology.

[11] See John Leadley Dagg, *Manual of Theology*, vol. 1 (Nashville: Southern Baptist Publication Society, 1859), 5.

[12] In this section, we have been arguing that what we believe should affect how we live. Other ethicists have attempted to highlight the relationship between ethics and theology, but they have reversed the order. That is, they propose that how we live precedes what we believe. See, for example, James William McClendon, *Ethics: Systematic Theology*, vol. 1 (Nashville, TN: Abingdon, 1986); Hauerwas, *Peaceable Kingdom: A Primer in Christian Ethics*, 16 and 54.

[13] By the term worldview, we mean something similar to what Charles Curran refers to as "stance" in Charles E. Curran, *The Catholic Moral Tradition Today: A Synthesis* (Washington, D.C.: Georgetown University, 1999). Likewise, Robin Lovin borrows the same term wherein he assumes that one's approach to moral problems springs from a set of beliefs that are generally shared by a particular community. In this regard, the "stance" is shared among Christians, and it includes beliefs about God and how God's presence directs the life of adherents to Christianity. See Robin Lovin, *An Introduction to Christian Ethics: Goals, Duties, and Virtues* (Nashville, TN: Abingdon, 2011).

[14] James W. Sire, *The Universe Next Door: A Basic Worldview Catalog* (Downers Grove: InterVarsity Press, 2009).

[15] Dara Lind, "The Ugly History of Racist Policing in America," *Vox Media*, July 7, 2016, 2016, https://www.vox.com/michael-brown-shooting-ferguson-mo/2014/8/19/6031759/ferguson-history-riots-police-brutality-civil-rights.

[16] For a better understanding of the official positions to various issues held by Hillary Clinton during the campaign, see responses posted on the Hillary Clinton website at https://www.hillaryclinton.com/issues/criminal-justice-reform.

[17] I recognize the ethical evaluation is more than simple presuppositions. Thus, one could have been raised to believe that one should trust police officers and still rightly conclude that the police are capable of racist and immoral motives.

[18] Robert C. Sproul, *Lifeviews: Make a Christian Impact on Culture and Society* (Grand Rapids: Fleming H. Revell, 1986), 16.

[19] For an excellent treatment for the philosophical foundations of worldviews, see James Porter Moreland, James Porter Moreland, and William Lane Craig,

Philosophical Foundations for a Christian Worldview (Downers Grove: InterVarsity Press, 2003).

[20] See Ronald H. Nash, *Life's Ultimate Questions: An Introduction to Philosophy* (Grand Rapids: Zondervan, 1999).

[21] Some philosophers might prefer to use the term "right" rather than "good." Rightness might better fit within the subdiscipline of axiology whereas goodness fits better into the field of value theory. I am not seeking to make these distinctions here, but rather to raise the types of questions that philosophical ethics might address.

[22] For a good discussion on the nature of moral conduct see Jochem Douma, *Responsible Conduct: Principles Ofchristian Ethics. Translated by Nelson D* (2003), 13-23.

[23] For Immanuel Kant, "ought" implies "can." See Immanuel Kant, *Religion within the Bounds of Bare Reason* (Hackett Publishing, 2009).

[24] For an excellent treatment of various historical authors who have used this approach, see David W. Jones, *An Introduction to Biblical Ethics* (Nashville, TN: B&H Academic, 2013).

[25] C. S. Lewis, *Mere Christianity* (MacMillan, 1943).

[26] God is the source of moral authority, and Scripture reflects how God exerts his authority.

Chapter 2

[1] Francis August Schaeffer, *He Is There and He Is Not Silent* (Carol Stream, IL: Tyndale House Publishers, 1972).

[2] Some authors might object to placing Kant within the camp of idealists, especially since some German Idealists such as Fichte, Schelling, and Hegel were reacting to their perceived failures of Kant. While he is a transcendental idealist, he might rightly be considered an empirical realist. In this section, I am merely broadly placing him within the idealist camp.

[3] For an excellent treatment of a biblical epistemology, see W. Andrew Hoffecker and G. K. Beale, "Biblical Epistemology: Revelation," in *Building a Christian Worldview*, ed. W. Andrew Holffeker and Gary Scott Smith (Phillipsburg, NJ: P&R, 1986), 193-216.

[4] For an excellent exposition of God's revelation, see Carl F. H. Henry, "God Who Speaks and Shows," in *God, Revelation, and Authority.* (Waco, TX: Word Books, 1999); Karl Barth, *Church Dogmatics: Doctrine of the Word of God*, vol. 1 (Edinburgh: T&T Clark, 1956). In Protestant theology during the twentieth century, theologians have vigorously debated the nature of God's revelation. One group advocated that revelation is primarily an encounter with God. Advocates of this

position include; Emil Brunner, *The Devine Imperative* (Louisville: Westminster Press, 1947); John Baillie, *Our Knowledge of God* (London: Oxford University Press, 1939); Cornelius Van Til, *The Protestant Doctrine of Scripture* (Phillipsburg: P&R, 1967). Advocates of Propositionalism, on the other hand, posit that God's revelation includes propositional truth and concepts. Advocates of this position include; Carl F. H. Henry, "God Who Speaks and Shows: Fifteen Theses, Part Two," in *God, Revelation, and Authority.* (Waco, TX: Word Books, 1999); Eward J. Carnell, *The Case for Biblical Christianity* (Grand Rapids: Eerdmans, 1969); James I. Packer, *God Has Spoken* (Downers Grove, IL: InterVarsity, 1979); James I. Packer, *God Speaks to Man: Revelation and the Bible* (Louisville: Westminster Press, 1965); James I. Packer, *Fundamentalism and the Word of God: Some Evangelical Principles* (Downers Grove: InterVarsity Fellowship, 1958).

⁵ For a good survey of the sources of revelation, see Millard J. Erickson, *Christian Theology* (Grand Rapids, MI: Baker Academic, 1998).

⁶ In current theological discourse, this claim may be considered controversial. Some distinguish between object revelation, personal revelation, and self-revelation.

⁷ David VanDrunen, *A Biblical Case for Natural Law* (Grand Rapids: Acton Institute, 2006), 7-22.

⁸ For a brief survey of major views on the image of God, see Erickson, 498-510.

⁹ VanDrunen, 12-13.

¹⁰ Certainly theologians differ on the degree to which they believe natural theology is useful. For an example of the use of natural theology for providing arguments for the existence of God via ontological, cosmological, and moral arguments, see William Lane Craig, *Reasonable Faith: Christian Truth and Apologetics* (Wheaton: Crossway, 2008), 77-125.Other philosophers, such as Reformed epistemologist Alvin Plantiga, reject natural theology as a grounds for God's existence. Rather, Plantiga believes that belief in God is itself a most basic belief. See Alvin Plantiga, *Two Dozen (or So) Theistic Arguments* (Cambridge: Cambridge University Press, 2007).

¹¹ For a good resource that demonstrates the character of God throughout the Pentateuch, see John K. Tarwater, *The Story of the Pentateuch: An Introduction to the Old Testament* (Cedarville: Coram Deo, 2015).

¹² The belief that God has made himself known does not imply that humanity can fully know God. Rather, Christianity has historically held that God specifically chose to reveal to some what was previously hidden and to reveal to all what nullifies everyone's excuse before him. Some have argued that this knowledge of God is merely analogical, supposing that this knowledge at no time coincides with God's knowledge. See James Douglas Baird, "Analogical Knowledge: A Systematic Interpretation of Cornelius Van Til's Theological Epistemology," *Mid-America*

Journal of Theology 26, no. 3 (2015): 77-103. Against this idea, however, Gordon Clark argued that the knowledge about God from the Bible must be seen as true knowledge of God, even if it is not exhaustive. He wrote: "If no proposition means to man what it means to God, so that God's knowledge and man's knowledge do not coincide at any single point, it follows by rigorous necessity that man can have no truth at all." See Gordon H. Clark, "The Bible as Truth," *Bibliotheca Sacra* 114 (1957): 163.

[13] While the church has largely affirmed this truth, that creation in the image of God includes rational and ethical features, this belief is not universally held. Karl Barth wrote, "The biblical witness makes no reference at all to the peculiar intellectual and moral talents and possibilities of man, to his reason and its determination and exercise" in Karl Barth, *Church Dogmatics: Doctrine of the Word of God*, vol. III (Edinburgh: T&T Clark, 1956), 185.

[14] Henry, *Christian Personal Ethics*, 150.

[15] Albert M. Wolters, *Creation Regained: Biblical Basics for a Reformational Worldview* (Grand Rapids: Eerdmans, 1985), 25.

[16] Jones, 34; Frame, 362-64; David Clyde Jones, *Biblical Christian Ethics* (Grand Rapids, MI: Baker Books, 1994), 72-6.

[17] See Hoffecker and Beale, in *Building a Christian Worldview*, 198-99.

[18] Often texts on ethics will present a number of ethical theories, like deontology, teleology, virtue ethics, justice and right, agency, and relativism, to name a few. In fact, some texts (especially secular texts for business ethics) present each of these theories as valid for approaching ethical questions. The perspective of these secular texts is that no one theory is superior to any other. Rather, it is what works best for the moral agent at the time. In this text, we do not want to present a list of theories. Rather, when a particular theory is relevant to the discussion, we will present it.

[19] For a good history of the Tuskegee study, see Susan M. Reverby, *Examining Tuskegee: The Infamous Syphilis Study and Its Legacy* (Chapel Hill: University of North Carolina Press, 2009).

[20] Centers for Disease Control and Prevention. U>S> Public Health Service Syphilis Study at Tuskegee. July 11, 2018. URL: https://www.cdc.gov/tuskegee/timeline.htm.

[21] For a discussion of principle monism, see Charles Pinches, "Principle Monism and Action Descriptions: Situationalism and Its Critics Revisited," *Modern Theology* 7, no. 3 (1991): 249-68.

[22] Joseph F. Fletcher, *Situation Ethics: The New Morality* (Louisville: Westminster John Knox Press, 1966).

[23]Immanuel Kant, *Groundwork of Metaphysic of Morals* (New Haven: Yale University Press, 2002), 82.

[24] Immanuel Kant, *Fundamental Principles of the Metaphysics of Morals* (Dover Publications, 2005), 38.

[25] For an interesting history of and approach to divine command theory in both Christian and Jewish faiths, see Michael J. Harris, *Divine Command Ethics: Jewish and Christian Perspectives* (Abingdon: Routledge, 2004); John E. Hare, *God's Command* (London: Oxford University Press, 2015). For a distinctly Christian view of it, see John Carnell, *An Introduction to Christian Apologetics* (Grand Rapids: Eerdmans, 1948).

[26] Henry, *Christian Personal Ethics*, 217.

[27] Plato, "Euthyphro," in *Plato: Complete Works*, ed. J. M. Cooper (Indianapolis, IN: Hackett, 1997), 10d.

[28] For a contemporary version of this dilemma, see K. Nielsen, *Ethics without God* (Amherst, NY: Prometheus Books, 1990).

[29] For an excellent presentation of this response to the dilemma, see Jones, 47-51.

[30] Geisler, 22.

[31] Henry, *Christian Personal Ethics*, 213.

[32] VanDrunen, 12-13.

[33] Murray, 177.

[34] Wayne Grudem provides strong evidence for how individuals can use various aspects of business activity to glorify God. Hence, these aspects represent means for moral evaluation. Interestingly, his primary argument rests on this truth: that we are created in God's image and we have a moral duty to imitate God. See Wayne Grudem, *Business for the Glory of God: The Bible's Teaching on the Moral Goodness of Business* (Wheaton: Crossway, 2003).

Chapter 3

[1] Jordan Yadoo, "U.S. Labor Unions," Bloomberg, last modified June 27, 2018, accessed November 9, 2019.

[2] Josh Bivens et al., "How Today's Unions Help Working People," Economic Policy Institute, last modified August 24, 2017, accessed November 9, 2019, 2019.

[3] For a survey to views on sanctification, see *Christian Spirituality: Five Views on Sanctification* (IVP Academic, 1988); Melvin Dieter et al., *Five Views on Sanctification* (Grand Rapids: Zondervan, 1987).

[4] See interesting debate between John Hare and Peter Singer at (https://www.youtube.com/watch?v=UU7sqi8iBBI.

[5] Graeme de Graff, *God and Morality* (London: SCM Press, 1973), 34.

[6] Ibid.

[7] For a discussion on the shortcomings of "quandary" ethics from this perspective, see Hauerwas, *Vision and Virtue: Essays in Christian Ethical Reflection.*

[8] It should be noted that many virtue ethicists do not always present their approach to ethics as an alternative to just deontology. Rather, they often argue against the entire notion of universal ethics. That is, they may oppose the existence of universal right actions, but they may also argue against right intentions, right outcomes (consequentialism), or even right relationships. Each of these alternative theories continue to center ethical discussion on conduct and universalize their conclusions. In contrast, many of these "ecclesial" ethicists focus on being and the community that is instrumental in forming the character of the individual. For a discussion of these alternatives, see Samuel Wells and Ben Quash, *Introducing Christian Ethics* (Hoboken, NJ: Wiley-Blackwell, 2010), 180-206.

[9] Aristotle, "Nichomachean Ethics," in *The Basic Works of Aristotle.*, ed. Richard McKeoon (Random House, 1941), 935-1126. Aristotle argued that not everyone would be swayed to live the good life by moral arguments. He bases his argument not on the fact that they were not intelligent enough, but rather, on the basis of their character. Therefore, he asks if virtue is in fact attainable. His answer is "yes." A person's nature can be altered by good influences. Robert George summarizes a political philosophy that stems from Aristotle as 'perfectionsim.' It is the idea that politics and good laws are concerned with helping people to lead morally upright and valuable lives. See Robert P George, *Making Men Moral: Civil Liberties and Public Morality* (Oxford: Clarendon Press, 1995). Likewise, narrative ethicists are arguing that the church is the *politics* where these good influences should be taught.

[10] Augustine, *Enchiridion on Faith, Hope and Love* (Regnery, 1996).

[11] As quoted in Wells and Quash, 194.

[12] Thomas Aquinas, *Summa Theologica*, trans. Fathers of the english Dominican Province (New York: Benziger Brothers, 1911 - 1925).

[13] Alasdair MacIntyre, *After Virtue* (Notre Dame, IN: University of Notre Dave, 1984).

[14] Ibid., 22..

[15] For a good summary of narrative and communitarian ethics, see Stanley J. Grenz, *The Moral Quest: Foundations of Christian Ethics* (Downers Grove: InterVarsity Press, 1997), 204-39.

16 Hauerwas himself usually avoids theological labels believing that they fail to capture fully one's position. AS such, je rejects calling himself a virtue ethicist, although most observers would place him squarely within that camp.

17 For a discussion of the relationship between "narrative" and morality, see Paul Nelson, *Narrative and Morality: A Theological Inquiry* (University Park: Pennsylvania State University Press, 1987).

18 Hauerwas, *Truthfulness and Tragedy.*

19 Hauerwas, *Peaceable Kingdom: A Primer in Christian Ethics*, 100.

20 Hauerwas, *The Community of Character*, 1.

21 Hauerwas, *Peaceable Kingdom: A Primer in Christian Ethics*, 17.

22 For an evangelical alternative, see Oliver O'Donovan, *The Desire of the Nations: Rediscovering the Roots of Political Theology* (Cambridge: Cambridge University Press, 1999). For O'Donovan, the sources of Christian ethics are available to everyone, and consequently, binding on everyone. As the title suggests, the "desire" of the nations is Jesus Christ.

23 See Frame. He considers discussion of virtue ethics under the rubric of the existential perspective for Christian ethics.

24 Scott B. Rae, *Moral Choices: An Introduction to Ethics* (New York: Harper Collins, 2009), 96.

25 For an excellent discussion on virtue ethics, see John E. Hare, *God and Morality: A Philosophical History* (Hoboken, NJ: Wiley-Blackwell, 2009), 250-51.

26 For a discussion of those who view virtue from a complementary or correspondence view, see Louis P. Pojman, *Ethical Theory: Classical and Contemporary Readings* (Belmont, CA: Wadsworth, 1995), 124-30.

27 For a philosophical discussion of this, see Alistair McFayden, *The Call to Personhood: A Christian Theory of the Individual in Social Relationships* (Cambridge: Cambridge University Press, 1990), 61-63.

28 Daniel J. Harrington and Keenan James F., *Paul and Virtue Ethics: Building Bridges between New Testament Studies and Moral Theology* (Lanham, MD: Rowman & Littlefield Publishers, 2010), 1..

29 In my doctoral studies in Christian ethics, I had the privilege of studying with an impressive theological professor named John Hammett. While his primary expertise was in systematic theology and the doctrine of the church in particular, he also possessed the capacity to speak deeply in other areas, such as the intersection of theology and ethics. My presentation of sanctification borrows deeply from his notes on this section.

[30] Perhaps the emphasis by evangelicals on justification being a moment and sanctification being a process stems from the desire to respond to Catholic teaching which treats justification as a process.

[31] David G. Peterson, *Possessed by God: A New Testament Theology of Sanctification and Holiness*, vol. 1 (Downers Grove: InterVarsity Press, 1995).

[32] See Wells and Quash, 194.

[33] See Duns Scotus, *On the Will & Morality*, trans. William A. Frank (Washington D.C.: Catholic University of America Press, 1997), 94-97.

[34] Jones, 113.

[35] John Bunyan, *The Pilgrim's Progress* (P.F. Collier & Son, 1909), 297.

[36] See Bryan Chapell, *Holiness by Grace:: Delighting in the Joy Tha Tis Our Strenghth* (Wheaton: Crossway, 2001), 8.; James I. Packer, *Rediscovering Holiness: Know the Fullness of Life with God* (Regal, 2009).

[37] For an excellent treatment of the role of grace in sanctification, see Jerry Bridges, *The Discipline of Grace: God's Role and Our Role in the Pursuit of Holiness* (Colorado: Navpress, 1994), 77-92.

[38] Ibid.

[39] For a detailed evaluation of these passages, see Michael Allen, *Sanctification* (Grand Rapids: Zondervan, 2017), 228ff.

[40] See John Owen, "The Mortification of Sin: The Necessity, Nature, and Means of It with a Resolution of Various Cases of Conscience Belonging to It," in *The Works of John Owen*, ed. William Goold (Johnstone & Hunter, 1850).

[41] In his book, Packer notes four disciplines through which one can cultivate the path to righteousness, all drawn from II Peter3:acceptance of facts, avoidance of folly, assimilation of food, and affirmation of fellowship. See Packer, *Rediscovering Holiness: Know the Fullness of Life with God*, 180-81..

[42] For a list, see Wayne A. Grudem, *Systematic Theology: An Introduction to Biblical Doctrine* (Grand Rapids: Zondervan, 2009), 951. Also, see Richard J. Foster, Emilie Griffin, and others, *Spiritual Classics: Selected Readings on the Twelve Spiritual Disciplines* (New York: Harper Collins, 2000). Dallas Willard, *The Spirit of the Disciplines-Reissue: Understanding How God Changes Lives* (Grand Rapids: Zondervan, 1990).

Chapter 4

[1] Jeremy Bentham, *An Introduction to the Principles of Morals and Legislation* (London: Clarendon Press, 1892), Chapter 2..

[2] Nash, 37.

[3] Aristotle, in *The Basic Works of Aristotle.*, 15.

[4] Jones, 17.

[5] Blaise Pascal, *Pensées* (Penguin, 1995), 51.

[6] Jonathan Edwards, *Christian Love and Its Fruits* (Sovereign Grace Publishers, 1971), 79.

[7] Augustine, *Of the Morals of the Catholic Church* (Peabody, MA: Hendrickson Publishers, 1994), 42.

[8] David K. Naugle, *Reordered Love, Reordered Lives* (Grand Rapids: William B. Eerdmans, 2008), 37.

[9] Augustine, *Of the Morals of the Catholic Church*, 42.

[10] Ibid.

[11] See the discussion on the Beatitudes in Willard, 97-98.

[12] This chart is from Naugle, 42.

[13] Stanley J Grenz, *The Moral Quest: Foundations of Christian Ethics* (Downers Grove: InterVarsity Press, 2000), 135.

[14] Augustine, *Concerning the Nature of the Good* (Random House, 1948).

[15] Augustine, *The City of God*, vol. 4 (Grand Rapids: Eerdmans, 1973), 8.8.

[16] Naugle, 45.

[17] William Cowper, *The Winter Walk at Noon* (Ward, Lock, & Co., Warwick House, 1882).

[18] Naugle, 51.

[19] For examples of authors who emphasize the future aspect of the kingdom, see C. H. Dodd, *The Parables of the Kingdom* (Nisbet, 1941); T. W. Manson, *Jesus the Messiah* (Hodder and Stoughton, 1943); T. W. Manson, *The Teaching of Jesus: Studies of Its Form and Content* (Cambridge: Cambridge University Press, 1959).

[20] See George Eldon Ladd, *A Theology of the New Testament* (Grand Rapids: William B. Eerdmans, 1974), 45-80.

[21] For examples of authors who emphasize the future aspect of the kingdom, see Albert Schweitzer, *They Mystery of the Kingdom of God: The Secret of Jesus' Messiahship and Passion*, trans. Walter Lowrie (New York: Dodd, Mead and Company, 1914); Albert Schweitzer, *The Quest of the Historical Jesus: A Critical Study of Its Progress from Reimarus to Wrede* (Macmillan, 1964); Johannes Weiss, *Jesus' Proclamation of the Kingdom of God* (Fortress Press, 1971).

[22] See, for example Gustaf Dalman, *The Words of Jesus* (Edinburgh: T & T Clark, 1902), 91-101; Donald Gutherie, *New Testament Theology* (Downers Grove:

InterVarsity Press, 1981), 408-29; George Eldon Ladd, *Jesus and the Kingdom: The Eschatology of Biblical Realism* (Harmondsworth: SPCK, 1966), 63.

23 Ladd, *A Theology of the New Testament*, 66.

24 R. E. O. White, *Christian Ethics* (Gracewing Publishing, 1994), 108.

25 Ladd, *A Theology of the New Testament*, 57.

26 Jones, 109-11.

27 B. Ramm, *Them He Glorified* (Grand Rapids: Eerdmans, 1963), 10.

28 For a discussion of how the term relates to the concept of shekhinah, see J. Abelson, *The Immanence of God* (Macmillan, 1912), 77-149.

29 John Piper, *Desring God* (Multnomah, 2003), 42.

30 Gutherie, 90-94.

31 For a discussion of the relationship of glory to Christian ethics, see Frame, 298-313; Jones, 17-36.

32 For a discussion of the roles that both God and man play in the kingdom, Bruce Chilton and J. I. H. McDonald, *Jesus and the Ethics of the Kingdom* (Grand Rapids: Eerdmans, 1987), 24-31; David P. Gushee and Glen H. Stassen, *Kingdom Ethics: Following Jesus in Contemporary Context* (Grand Rapids: Eerdmans, 2016), 12-19.

Made in the USA
Monee, IL
08 September 2020